947.085 SMI

L

The Russian Revolution: A Very Short Introduction

'Written with verve, this book is a triumph of compression: it will immediately establish itself as the best short introduction to the subject.'
Simon Dixon, University of Leeds

'Written by one of the very best historians of early 20th-century Russia, Steve Smith's *Russian Revolution* is now the best short overview of the Russian experience from the world war to the end of the 1920s, an intelligent and interpretively fair introduction to the social and political history of these complex and important years.'
Mark Steinberg, University of Illinois

VERY SHORT INTRODUCTIONS are for anyone wanting a stimulating and accessible way in to a new subject. They are written by experts, and have been published in 25 languages worldwide.

The series began in 1995, and now represents a wide variety of topics in history, philosophy, religion, science, and the humanities. Over the next few years it will grow to a library of around 200 volumes – a Very Short Introduction to everything from ancient Egypt and Indian philosophy to conceptual art and cosmology.

Very Short Introductions available now:

ANCIENT PHILOSOPHY
  Julia Annas
THE ANGLO-SAXON AGE
  John Blair
ANIMAL RIGHTS
  David DeGrazia
ARCHAEOLOGY· Paul Bahn
ARISTOTLE Jonathan Barnes
AUGUSTINE Henry Chadwick
BARTHES Jonathan Culler
THE BIBLE John Riches
BUDDHA Michael Carrithers
BUDDHISM Damien Keown
CLASSICS Mary Beard and
  John Henderson
CLAUSEWITZ Michael Howard
CONTINENTAL PHILOSOPHY
  Simon Critchley
COSMOLOGY Peter Coles
DARWIN Jonathan Howard
DESCARTES Tom Sorell
DRUGS Leslie Iversen
EIGHTEENTH-CENTURY
  BRITAIN Paul Langford
THE EUROPEAN UNION
  John Pinder
THE FRENCH REVOLUTION
  William Doyle
FREUD Anthony Storr
GALILEO Stillman Drake
GANDHI Bhikhu Parekh
HEGEL Peter Singer

HEIDEGGER Michael Inwood
HINDUISM Kim Knott
HISTORY John H. Arnold
HOBBES Richard Tuck
HUME A. J. Ayer
INDIAN PHILOSOPHY
  Sue Hamilton
INTELLIGENCE Ian J. Deary
ISLAM Malise Ruthven
JUDAISM Norman Solomon
JUNG Anthony Stevens
KANT Roger Scruton
KIERKEGAARD Patrick Gardiner
THE KORAN Michael Cook
LITERARY THEORY
  Jonathan Culler
LOGIC Graham Priest
MACHIAVELLI Quentin Skinner
MARX Peter Singer
MEDIEVAL BRITAIN
  John Gillingham and
  Ralph A. Griffiths
MUSIC Nicholas Cook
NIETZSCHE Michael Tanner
NINETEENTH-CENTURY
  BRITAIN Christopher Harvie and
  H. C. G. Matthew
PAUL E. P. Sanders
PHILOSOPHY Edward Craig
POLITICS Kenneth Minogue
PSYCHOLOGY Gillian Butler and
  Freda McManus

ROMAN BRITAIN
  Peter Salway
ROUSSEAU   Robert Wokler
RUSSELL   A. C. Grayling
RUSSIAN LITERATURE
  Catriona Kelly
THE RUSSIAN REVOLUTION
  S. A. Smith
SCHOPENHAUER
  Christopher Janaway
SHAKESPEARE   Germaine Greer

SOCIAL AND CULTURAL
  ANTHROPOLOGY
  John Monaghan and Peter Just
SOCIOLOGY   Steve Bruce
SOCRATES   C. C. W. Taylor
STUART BRITAIN   John Morrill
THEOLOGY   David F. Ford
THE TUDORS   John Guy
TWENTIETH-CENTURY
  BRITAIN   Kenneth O. Morgan
WITTGENSTEIN   A. C. Grayling

Available soon:

AFRICAN HISTORY
  John Parker and Richard Rathbone
ANCIENT EGYPT   Ian Shaw
ARCHITECTURE
  Andrew Ballantyne
ART HISTORY   Dana Arnold
ASTRONOMY   Michael Hoskin
THE BRAIN   Michael O'Shea
BRITISH POLITICS
  Anthony Wright
CAPITALISM   James Fulcher
CHAOS   Leonard Smith
CHRISTIAN ART   Beth Williamson
CHRISTIANITY   Linda Woodhead
CITIZENSHIP   Richard Bellamy
CLASSICAL ARCHITECTURE
  Robert Tavernor
CLONING   Arlene Klotzko
THE COLD WAR   Robert McMahon
CONTEMPORARY ART
  Julian Stallabrass
THE CRUSADES
  Christopher Tyerman
CRYPTOGRAPHY
  Fred Piper and Sean Murphy
DADA AND SURREALISM
  David Hopkins
DEMOCRACY   Bernard Crick
DESIGN   John Heskett
DREAMING   J. Allan Hobson

THE EARTH   Martin Redfern
ECONOMICS   Partha Dasgupta
THE ELEMENTS   Philip Ball
EMPIRE   Stephen Howe
EVOLUTION   .
  Brian and Deborah Charlesworth
FASCISM   Kevin Passmore
FILM   Mark Jancovich
THE FIRST WORLD WAR
  Michael Howard
FREE WILL   Thomas Pink
FUNDAMENTALISM
  Malise Ruthven
HIEROGLYPHS   Penelope Wilson
HIROSHIMA   B. R. Tomlinson
IDEOLOGY   Michael Freeden
INTERNATIONAL RELATIONS
  Paul Wilkinson
LINGUISTICS   Peter Matthews
MANDELA   Tom Lodge
MATHEMATICS   Timothy Gowers
MEDICAL ETHICS   Tony Hope
THE MIND   Martin Davies
MODERN IRELAND   Senia Pašeta
MOLECULES   Philip Ball
NORTHERN IRELAND
  Marc Mulholland
PERCEPTION   Richard Gregory
PHILOSOPHY OF RELIGION
  Jack Copeland and Diane Proudfoot

PHILOSOPHY OF SCIENCE
  Samir Okasha
PHOTOGRAPHY   Steve Edwards
PLATO   Julia Annas
POSTCOLONIALISM
  Robert Young
POSTMODERNISM
  Christopher Butler
POSTSTRUCTURALISM
  Catherine Belsey
PREHISTORY   Chris Gosden
QUANTUM THEORY
  John Polkinghorne
THE RAJ   Denis Judd
THE RENAISSANCE   Jerry Brotton

RENAISSANCE ART
  Geraldine Johnson
SCHIZOPHRENIA
  Chris Frith and Eve Johnstone
THE SECOND WORLD WAR
  Joanna Bourke
THE SPANISH CIVIL WAR
  Helen Graham
SPINOZA   Roger Scruton
TERRORISM
  Charles Townshend
TRAGEDY   Adrian Poole
THE TWENTIETH-CENTURY
  Martin Conway
WORLD MUSIC   Philip Bohlman

For more information visit our web site

www.oup.co.uk/vsi

S. A. Smith

THE RUSSIAN REVOLUTION

A Very Short Introduction

OXFORD
UNIVERSITY PRESS

OXFORD
UNIVERSITY PRESS

Great Clarendon Street, Oxford OX2 6DP

Oxford University Press is a department of the University of Oxford.
It furthers the University's objective of excellence in research, scholarship,
and education by publishing worldwide in

Oxford New York

Auckland Bangkok Buenos Aires Cape Town Chennai
Dar es Salaam Delhi Hong Kong Istanbul Karachi Kolkata
Kuala Lumpur Madrid Melbourne Mexico City Mumbai Nairobi
São Paulo Shanghai Singapore Taipei Tokyo Toronto

and an associated company in Berlin

Oxford is a registered trade mark of Oxford University Press
in the UK and in certain other countries

Published in the United States
by Oxford University Press Inc., New York

© Steve Smith 2002

The moral rights of the author have been asserted

Database right Oxford University Press (maker)

First published as a Very Short Introduction 2002

British Library Cataloguing in Publication Data

Data available

Library of Congress Cataloging in Publication Data

Data available

ISBN 0-19-285395-3

3 5 7 9 10 8 6 4 2

Typeset by RefineCatch Ltd, Bungay, Suffolk
Printed in Spain by Book Print S. L., Barcelona

Contents

List of illustrations   viii

List of maps   x

Introduction   1

1   From February to October   5

2   Civil war and the foundation of the Bolshevik regime   40

3   War Communism   72

4   NEP: politics and the economy   100

5   NEP: society and culture   129

Conclusion   157

Further reading   169

Index   173

List of illustrations

1 International Women's Day,
   8 March 1917   7
   David King Collection

2 A political demonstration in
   Petrograd, 1917   15
   Hulton Archive

3 *Who Has Forgotten His
   Debt to His Motherland?*
   Merchants address this
   question to a downcast
   soldier. The inscription
   reads 'Little is given, much
   is exacted.'   18
   A. Nenarokov, *An Illustrated History of
   the Great October Socialist Revolution*
   (Moscow, 1987)

4 Russian soldiers
   demonstrating in
   Petrograd, April 1917   23
   David King Collection

5 Troops firing on Bolsheviks
   in July demonstrations   25
   David King Collection

6 General Kornilov   33
   David King Collection

7 Red Guards in
   Ekaterinburg   36
   Hulton Archive

8 Trotsky reviewing the
   Red troops during
   the Civil War, 1917   50
   David King Collection

9 Baron Wrangel leaves
   Russia   52
   David King Collection

10 Derailed train with two Red
   Army soldiers   66
   David King Collection

11 A country market in the 1920s 77
David King Collection

12 A food requisition group, 1918 79
David King Collection

13 A child's cartoon. The caption reads 'A Bolshevik is a person who doesn't want there to be any more burzhui.' 81
A. Nenarokov, *An Illustrated History of the Great October Socialist Revolution* (Moscow, 1987)

14 Famine 1921–2 84
David King Collection

15 Krupskaia and Lenin, Gorki, 1922 110
David King Collection

16 Anti-capitalist demonstration, 1920s 132
David King Collection

17 Children's demonstration 136
David King Collection

18 The model of Vladimir Tatlin's *Monument to the Third International* 151
David King Collection

19 Altman's design for Palace Square 152
David King Collection

20 Constructivist poster design for Dziga Vertov's film, *The Eleventh* 154
David King Collection

21 Demonstration: 'Let us direct our path towards the shining life' 158
Tolstoy, *Street Art of the Revolution, Festivals and Celebrations in Russia 1918–23* (Thames and Hudson, 1990)

22 Red Square caricatures 166
David King Collection

List of maps

1   European Russia on the eve of 1917   4

2   The Soviet state at the end of the civil war   58

Introduction

The Russian Revolution of 1917 saw the overthrow of the tsarist autocracy in February and the seizure of power by the Bolshevik party in October. The Bolsheviks proceeded to establish the world's first Communist state on a territory covering one-sixth of the globe, that stretched from the Arctic to the Black Sea, from the Baltic to the Far East. Their revolution proved to be the most consequential event of the 20th century, inspiring communist movements and revolutions across the world, notably in China, provoking a reaction in the form of fascism, and after 1945 having a profound influence on many anti-colonial movements and shaping the architecture of international relations through the Cold War. This book sets out to provide for the reader coming to the subject for the first time an analytical narrative of the main events and developments from 1917 to 1929, when I. V. Stalin launched his 'revolution from above', bringing crash industrialization and the forced collectivization of agriculture to the Soviet Union. It seeks to explain how and why revolution broke out in 1917; how the Bolsheviks came to power and established a regime; and how, finally, that regime evolved into a gruesome form of totalitarianism. The book attends to the ideals and aspirations that animated the contenders for power and the issues and conflicts with which they had to grapple. But it seeks to go beyond politics narrowly defined. The October Revolution set out to do nothing less than destroy an entire social system and replace it with a society superior to anything that had existed hitherto in human history. The book explores the far-reaching reverberations of that project on the economy, peasant life, work, structures of government, the family, empire, education, law and order, and the Church. More particularly, it explores what the revolution meant – the hopes it inspired and the disappointments it brought – for different groups such as peasants, workers, soldiers, non-Russian nationalities, the intelligentsia, men and women, and young people. The perspective is that of the social historian, but the central concern is political: to understand how ordinary people experienced and participated in the overthrow of one structure of domination and how they experienced and resisted the gradual emergence of a new one. Each chapter is punctuated with a couple of quotations from documents that have come to light since the fall of the Soviet Union; they are intended to give a flavour of the range of responses of those who found themselves caught up in the revolution.

In 1991 the state to which the Russian Revolution gave rise collapsed, allowing historians to see the history of the Russian Revolution in its entirety for the first time. That shift in perspective, together with the passing of the 20th century, suggests that it is a good time to reflect more philosophically on the meaning of the revolution. Somewhat unusually for an introductory text, therefore, it touches on certain fundamental questions, such as the role of ideology and human agency in revolution, the interplay of emancipatory and enslaving elements in the Bolshevik project, and the influence of Russian culture on the development of the Soviet Union. The book incorporates advances in research and interpretation made by western scholars since the 1980s – particularly in the sphere of social and cultural history – and the work of Russian scholars who were freed from the trammels of Soviet censorship in 1991. The introductory nature of this text and the tight constraints of space preclude the standard scholarly apparatus of reference. I thus wish to apologise to – and thank – the many specialists on whose work I have drawn without customary acknowledgement.

Readers should note that up to 1 February 1918 dates are given in the old style. On that date the Bolsheviks changed from the Julian calendar, which was 13 days behind that of the West, to the western calendar. The October seizure of power (24–5 October 1917) thus took place on 6–7 November 1917, according to the western calendar.

Warmest thanks go to Cathy Merridale and Chris Ward who read the manuscript and offered characteristically astute and helpful comments. Needless to say, responsibility for any errors remains my own.

Introduction

Map 1. European Russia on the eve of 1917

Chapter 1
From February to October

On 23 February 1917 thousands of female textile-workers and housewives took to the streets of Petrograd, the Russian capital, to protest about the bread shortage and to mark International Women's Day. The following day, more than 200,000 workers were on strike and demonstrators marched from the outlying districts into the city centre, hurling rocks and lumps of ice at police as they went. By 25 February, students and members of the middle classes had joined the protesters, who now bore placards proclaiming 'Down with the War' and 'Down with the Tsarist Government'. On 26 February, soldiers from the garrison were ordered to fire on the crowds, killing hundreds. The next morning, the Volynskii regiment mutinied, its example quickly followed by other units. By 1 March, 170,000 soldiers swarmed among the insurgents, who were by this stage attacking prisons and police stations, arresting officials, and destroying tsarist 'emblems of slavery'. A revolution had broken out, but not until 27 February did any of the revolutionary parties manage to give leadership to it. Looking back to the revolution of 1905, the moderate wing of the Russian Social Democratic and Labour Party (RSDLP), the Mensheviks, called on workers and soldiers to elect delegates to a soviet, or council. Thus was born the Petrograd Soviet of Workers' and Soldiers' Deputies.

On the same day, members of the duma, or parliament, alarmed at disorders on the street, resolved to capitalize on the crisis in order to extract political concessions from the tsar. Significantly, they persuaded the army generals that nothing short of Tsar Nicholas II's abdication could ensure the successful continuance of the war. On 2 March members of the duma went ahead without a formal mandate and established a provisional, or temporary, government. The next day, since his brother could not be persuaded to take the throne, Nicholas abdicated and the 300-year-old Romanov dynasty came to an ignominious end. In 1905 the autocracy had withstood the revolutionary movement for 12 months; in February 1917, deprived of the support from the army, it survived for less than 12 days.

The collapse of the autocracy was rooted in a crisis of modernization. From the 1860s, and particularly from the 1890s, the government tried hard to keep abreast militarily and economically of the major European powers by modernizing Russia's economy. By 1913 Russia had become the fifth largest industrial power in the world. However, economic modernization was carried out in an external and internal environment that was deeply threatening to the autocracy. The empire was challenged by Japan in the Far East, leading to war in 1904; by Germany in central Europe and the Ottoman empire; and in the decade up to 1914 by instability in the Balkans. Internally, the modernization was menaced by the deep social tensions that scarred this backward, poverty-stricken country. The government hoped that it could carry out modernization whilst maintaining tight control over society. Yet the effect of industrialization, urbanization, internal migration, and the emergence of new social classes was to set in train forces that served to erode the foundations of the autocratic state.

The difficulties of modernization were nowhere clearer than in agriculture. On the eve of the revolution, three-quarters of Russia's population was still engaged in farming. Russia had been the last country in Europe to abolish serfdom, but the emancipation of 1861 had left peasants feeling cheated, since the landed gentry kept roughly one-sixth of the land – usually the best-quality land – and since the peasants

1. International Women's Day, 8 March 1917

had to pay for the land they received at a price above its market value. Between 1860 and 1914 the population of the empire grew rapidly from 74 million to 164 million, putting intense pressure on land resources, especially in the central and Volga provinces where the black earth was very fertile. The average peasant allotment shrank by one-third between 1861 and 1900. The fact that by 1917 the landed gentry had lost almost half their land – much of it sold to peasants – and rented most of the remaining land to peasants, made little difference to how peasants felt.

In spite of increasing land hunger, peasant living standards were actually rising very slowly after 1891, although not in the central black-earth provinces. The rapid expansion of the market – stimulated by the construction of railways – allowed peasants to supplement their income from farming with work in industry, trade, handicrafts, or on the farms of the well-to-do; it also stimulated commercial production of grain, making Russia the world's leading grain exporter by 1913. Yet the average peasant still lived a life of poverty, deprivation, and oppression, one index of which was that infant mortality was the highest in Europe. Moreover, notwithstanding the expansion of commercial farming, agriculture continued to be technically primitive, based on the three-field system and strip farming, with little use of fertilizer or machinery. In spite of clear signs that agriculture was beginning to commercialize, then, the agrarian system as a whole remained backward and the peasantry deeply alienated.

By 1914, 18% of the empire's population was urban. Towns grew rapidly, mainly as a result of peasant migration, and this put immense strain on the urban infrastructure. Overcrowding, high rents, and appalling squalor were the norm in the big cities. Incompetent municipal authorities, dogged by an inadequate tax base (there was no income tax until 1916), proved unable to cope with rising levels of disease and mortality. St Petersburg – which changed its name to Petrograd during the First World War – enjoyed the dubious distinction of being the most unhealthy capital in Europe. In 1908 more than 14,000 people died in a cholera epidemic. In the burgeoning towns, the traditional system of social estates, which defined the fiscal and military obligations of the tsar's subjects according to whether they belonged to the nobility, clergy, merchantry, or peasantry, was breaking down. New classes, such as the professional and commercial middle classes, the industrial bourgeoisie, and the working class, were emerging, posing demands on the system that it was not designed to accommodate.

As early as the 1830s a social group had emerged that stood outside the system of social estates. This was the characteristically Russian group known as the intelligentsia, defined less by its socio-economic position than by its critical stance towards the autocracy. Liberal and socialist in its politics, it did much in the course of 70 years to erode the legitimacy of the autocracy, not least by providing a steady flow of members to the terrorist and socialist groups that struggled to overthrow the system by violent revolution. By the turn of the 20th century, the intelligentsia was becoming less clearly defined, as professional and commercial middle classes emerged, as the middle and upper ranks of the bureaucracy became professionalized, and as mass commercial culture developed. The professional and commercial middle classes had been slow to develop in Russia, but by the time revolution broke out in 1905 they were making their mark on society. A civil society was emerging, manifest in the professional associations of lawyers, doctors, and teachers, in voluntary associations of a charitable or reformist type, in the expansion of universities, and especially in the explosion of publishing.

In 1905 the intelligentsia and the middle classes together campaigned for the autocracy to give them civil and political rights and establish a constitutional political order. They thus played a role similar to that which in western Europe had been performed by a more economically defined bourgeoisie. In Russia, however, the capitalist class was politically unassertive, deeply segmented by region and branch of industry, and tied to the traditional merchant estate. Industrialists in key sections of the mining, metallurgy, and engineering industries relied on the state for orders, subsidies, and preferential tariffs, and showed little will to confront it.

The growth of an industrial proletariat posed a challenge of a different kind. In 1917 there were still only 3.6 million workers in Russia's factories and mines, yet their concentration in particular regions and in relatively large enterprises gave them a political clout out of all proportion to their numbers. Mainly recruited from the peasants – 'snatched from the plough and hurled into the factory furnace' in L. D. Trotsky's memorable phrase – they varied considerably in the extent to which they were tied to the land, involved in urban culture, educated, and skilled. There were big differences, for example, between the skilled metalworkers of Vyborg district in Petrograd, the textile-workers of the Moscow industrial region, and the workers from the mining settlements of the Urals. Nevertheless the proportion of workers who had severed their ties with the village and who were becoming socialized into the urban-industrial environment was increasing. Towns provided workers with cultural opportunities, such as evening classes, clubs, libraries, theatres, and mass entertainment, and exposed them to the subversive political ideas of Social Democrats and Socialist Revolutionaries. The wretched conditions in which workers lived, the drudgery of their work, and their pitiful wages heightened their sense of separateness not only from the government but from privileged society in general.

Following the general strike of 1905, the autocracy conceded limited legalization of trade unions, but employers showed little desire to reform the authoritarian system of industrial relations. Moreover, since the response of the authorities to strikes and demonstrations was to send in police and Cossacks, workers were easily politicized, seeing in the state and capitalists a single mechanism of oppression. Deprived of the chance to pursue improvement by gradualistic means, Russian workers became the most strike-prone in Europe: in 1905–6 and again in 1912–14, the annual number of strikers was equivalent to almost three-quarters of the factory workforce.

In October 1905, under intense pressure from the 'all-nation struggle' of the labour movement and the middle-class and gentry opposition, Nicholas II, in the October Manifesto, conceded an elected legislature, or duma, plus substantial civil rights. The revolution had exposed the vulnerability of the autocracy, but it also rekindled the reformist energies of the bureaucracy. Nowhere was this more apparent than in Prime Minister P. A. Stolypin's bold legislation to allow peasants to separate from the agricultural commune by consolidating their land holdings into private plots. Many of the middle classes, alarmed by the extent of worker and peasant insurgency, were ready to work with a constitutional monarchy in the interests of social reform. Yet the massive unrest in the countryside in 1906–7, which saw the burning and looting of gentry estates, together with the radicalism shown by peasants in elections to the first and second dumas in 1906 and 1907, demonstrated the perils of controlled modernization.

Once the revolutionary storm had died down, Stolypin in June 1907 launched a 'coup' against the duma, limiting its power and drastically reducing peasant representation. Thereafter the regime became steadily more isolated. The middle classes continued to support the faltering efforts at reform, but felt betrayed by the way in which Nicholas and his ministers clawed back the concessions granted in the October Manifesto. Workers, needless to say, remained profoundly alienated from the regime and from the wealthy and privileged classes. More worryingly, the autocracy was losing its traditional supporters. The 1905 revolution had destroyed peasant loyalty to their 'little father' the tsar, and the Stolypin reforms failed by 1914 to create a layer of conservative farmers who might have provided a new base for the regime. The authority of the Orthodox Church was in decline and the once liberal gentry, debt-ridden and aghast at peasant insurgency, harried the bureaucracy for failing to protect its interests. Finally, the project of orderly modernization was also threatened by the appearance of nationalism among the non-Russian peoples of the empire.

In 1906 the tsarist state was weak but not necessarily doomed. Orderly modernization in a world of intensifying competition between empire-nations and in a society torn by social conflict was never going to be easy. But it might have succeeded had the resolve of the regime not been undermined by the unwillingness of the tsar to tolerate any weakening of his authority. The tsar sincerely believed that, as God's appointed representative, he did not have the right to compromise his power. The omens were evident in the first line of Basic Law of 1906, which ostensibly enshrined a constitutional monarchy: 'To the All-Russian Emperor belongs the Supreme Autocratic Power.' Consequently, by 1907, with the revolutionary crisis at an end, the regime began to retreat from its commitment to open up the political process to new social forces. By 1913–14, Russia's cities were once again awash with conflict. Nevertheless the autocracy collapsed not because of its unwillingness to reform, nor even because of the intrinsic contradictions of controlled modernization, acute though these had become, but because of the First World War.

The war marked a watershed in Europe's history, destroying empires, discrediting liberal democracy, preparing the way for the totalitarian politics of the 1920s and 1930s. It exposed all the belligerents to the severest of tests and found the Russian autocracy wanting. The war had a devastating impact on the empire. Over 14 million men were mobilized; about 67 million people in the western provinces came under enemy occupation; over 6 million were forcibly displaced, of whom half a million were Jews expelled from front-line areas. The eastern front was less static than the western, but neither side was able to make a decisive breakthrough and offensives proved hugely costly. Perhaps 3.3 million died or were lost without trace – a higher mortality than any other belligerent power (although Germany had a higher number of counted dead) – and the total number of casualties reached over 8 million. The mass slaughter and seething hatreds to which the war gave rise fatally compromised the chances of democracy after the autocracy had been overthrown.

> They drove us and we went. Where was I going and why? To kill the Germans! But why? I didn't know. I arrived in the trenches, which were terrifying and appalling. I listened as our company commander beat a soldier, beat him about the head with a whip. Blood poured from the poor man's head. Well, I thought, as soon as he begins to beat me, I'll skewer him with my bayonet and be taken prisoner. I thought who really is my enemy: the Germans or the company commander? I still couldn't see the Germans, but here in front of me was the commander. The lice bit me in the trenches. I was overcome with dejection. And then as we were retreating I was taken prisoner.
>
> F. Starunov, a peasant conscript in the First World War

Russian soldiers fought valiantly and generally successfully against Turks and Austrians, but proved no match for the German army in matters of organization, discipline, and leadership. General Brusilov's offensive of June 1916, however, testified to the resilience of the Russian soldiers and by that stage the army had overcome the shortage of shells that had dogged its first months in the field. When the February Revolution came, it was not as the result of military defeat, or even of war weariness, but as the result of the collapse of public confidence in the government.

In November 1915, after a disastrous first year of battle, Nicholas took personal command of the armed forces. Though diligent, he had neither the ability nor imagination to coordinate the external and the home fronts and stubbornly resisted calls from the duma for a 'government of public confidence'. The empress Alexandra interfered erratically in government and her devotion to the peasant holy man, Rasputin, set rumours flying of sexual shenanigans and treason by 'dark forces' at court. These alienated not only the common people but also many officials, generals, and aristocrats from what was perceived to be a 'pro-German' court. Meanwhile the bureaucracy, never known for its efficiency, buckled under the punishing demands of 'total war'. So disgusted were the middle classes with the ineptitude of the official supply organs that the Union of Towns and the Union of Zemstvos, the organs of local government in the countryside, took on the task of organizing supplies and services for the army. It proved impossible, however, to mobilize transport, industry, and fuel for the army without undermining the civilian economy.

The government financed the war by raising taxes and foreign loans and by massively increasing the amount of paper currency in circulation. The result was a vast increase in government debt and rising inflation. Prices tripled between 1914 and 1916, while wages doubled. Industrialists made record profits, while workers struggled to make ends meet. By 1916 the intensity of industrial strikes again approached the level of the pre-war period; in January–February 1917 more workers participated in political strikes than in 1913. By the winter, the cities were facing an acute food shortage in a country glutted with food. Asked in January 1917 by Sir George Buchanan, the British Ambassador, how he proposed to regain his subjects' confidence, Nicholas retorted: 'Do you mean that I am to regain the confidence of my people, or that they are to regain mine?'

The meanings of the revolution

The February Revolution gave rise to a short-lived mood of national unity and optimism. Liberty and democracy were the order of the day. Overnight everyone was transformed from a subject into a citizen, all agreeing that they must organize in order to realize their freedom. The extraordinary euphoria of public life was captured by V. I. Lenin's wife,

2. A political demonstration in Petrograd, 1917

Nadezda Krupskaia, upon her return to Russia in early April: 'Everywhere people stood about in knots, arguing heatedly and discussing the latest events. Discussion that nothing could interrupt!' Yet from the first, the scope of the revolution was in dispute. For the reluctant revolutionaries of the Provisional Government the overthrow of the tsar was an act of national self-preservation driven by the need to bring victory in war. For the lower classes, liberty and democracy meant nothing short of a social revolution that would bring about the complete destruction of the old structure of authority and the construction of a new way of life in accordance with their ideas of justice and freedom. It was only a matter of time before the social contradictions masked by the common political language would become exposed.

Nine million soldiers and sailors hailed the downfall of the tsar, seeing the revolution as a signal to overthrow the oppressive command structure in the armed forces. Tyrannical officers were removed and sometimes lynched (about 50 officers were murdered by the sailors of

15

Kronstadt). Insisting that they were citizens of a free Russia, soldiers demanded the right to form committees from the company level upwards to represent their interests. This demand was conceded by the Petrograd Soviet on 1 March, when it passed Order No. 1, the most radical act it ever carried out. General M. V. Alekseev condemned it as 'the means by which the army I command will be destroyed'. Yet the committees were dominated by more educated elements who had little intention of sabotaging the operational effectiveness of the army. In spring at least, democratization did not mean the disintegration of the army as a fighting force. The mood of the soldiers was characterized by Lenin as one of 'revolutionary defencism', by which he meant that soldiers would only fight to defend the gains of the revolution against Austro-German militarism. Hopes for a rapid peace settlement, however, ran high and no one could be confident that the army would continue to fight indefinitely. In particular, it was not clear that the army would go on the attack.

Industrial workers were the most organized and strategically positioned of all social groups in 1917. Upon their return to work, following the end of the general strike, they, too, set about dismantling 'autocracy' on the shop floor. Hated foremen and administrators were driven out, the old rule books were torn up, and factory committees were formed, especially among the skilled metalworkers, to represent workers' interests to management. Everywhere they demanded an eight-hour working day and wage rises to compensate for wartime inflation, both demands conceded with considerable reluctance by employers. The factory committees took on a wide range of functions, including guarding factory property, overseeing hiring and firing, labour discipline, and organizing food supplies. By October two-thirds of enterprises with 200 or more workers had such committees. Had economic and political conditions been more favourable, it is possible that they might have become part of a corporatist system of industrial relations, taking joint responsibility with employers for production. Meanwhile more slowly, trade unions also revived, taking particular responsibility for wage negotiations. By October they had over 2 million members, organized by industry rather than craft.

The soviets were the principal organ of political expression for the workers and soldiers. Some 700 soviets sprang up in March and April, embracing around 200,000 deputies by summer. By October there were 1,429 soviets, of which 455 were soviets of peasants' deputies. Peasant soviets, however, did not really get off the ground until the end of 1917. Soviets saw themselves as organs of the 'revolutionary democracy' – a bloc comprising workers, soldiers, and peasants, and occasionally stretching (as in Omsk) to include representatives of ethnic minorities and even teachers, journalists, lawyers, and doctors. Their basic principle was that they were directly elected by those they represented and directly accountable to them. During the spring and summer, the moderate socialists, the Mensheviks and Socialist Revolutionaries (SRs), were the leading force in the soviets, because their brand of inclusive politics was most in tune with the popular mood. The moderate socialists saw the function of the soviets as being to exercise 'control' over local government in the interests of the revolutionary democracy; but in practice many local soviets quickly took on administrative responsibilities in matters as various as food and fuel supply, education and culture, and law and order. At the beginning of June at the First All-Russian Congress of Soviets, out of 777 delegates, 285 were SRs and 248 were Mensheviks. The Congress brought into being a national soviet centre, the Central Executive Committee (CEC), controlled by Mensheviks and SRs, that became a bastion of support for the Provisional Government.

The peasants too responded warmly to the February Revolution. Few mourned the passing of the Romanov dynasty and thousands of resolutions were passed by village communities, applauding the fact that peasants were now citizens and demanding that the social order be reconstructed on the basis of democracy, justice, and equality. Peasant

3. *Who Has Forgotten His Debt to His Motherland?* Merchants address this question to a downcast soldier. The inscription reads 'Little is given, much is exacted.'

resolutions expressed hope that the war would soon be over, but their principal aspiration was to redress the wrong done to them in 1861 by redistributing the gentry's estates. Although there were only about 100,000 landlord families by 1917, few countries in the world still had estates as large as those in Russia. In the eyes of the peasants, the gentry had no right to these estates since they did not work them. In the moral universe of the peasantry it was an article of faith that only those who made the land productive had a right to it. In one of Tolstoy's fables, the peasants of a village judge strangers by the state of their hands: only if their palms are calloused will they take them in.

Dual power

The two forces that brought down the monarchy – the mass movement of workers and soldiers and the middle-class parliamentary opposition – became institutionalized in the new political set-up, the Petrograd

Soviet keeping a watchful eye over the Provisional Government. The government, headed by Prince G. E. Lvov, a landowner with a long record of service to the zemstvos, was broadly representative of professional and business interests. It was liberal, even mildly populist, in its politics; the only organized force within it was the Kadet party, once a liberal party but now evolving rapidly in the direction of conservative nationalism. In its manifesto of 2 March, the government pledged to implement a far-reaching programme of civil and political rights and to convoke a Constituent Assembly. Significantly, it said nothing about the burning issues of war and land. The government, which had no popular mandate, saw its principal task as being to oversee the election of a Constituent Assembly, which would determine the shape of the future polity. It believed that only such an assembly had the authority to resolve such pressing issues as land redistribution.

The Petrograd Soviet enjoyed the real attributes of power since it controlled the army, transport, and communications, as well as vital means of information. It also had a popular mandate insofar as 1,200 deputies were elected to it within the first week. A few Bolsheviks, anarchists, and others pressed the Soviet to assume full power, but the moderate socialist intellectuals who controlled its executive committee believed that this was not appropriate to a revolution whose character they defined as 'bourgeois', i.e. as destined to bring about democracy and capitalist development in Russia rather than socialism. In addition, they feared that any attempt to assert their authority would provoke 'counter-revolution'. Consequently, they agreed to support but not to join the 'bourgeois' Provisional Government, so long as it did not override the interests of the people. The radical lawyer A. F. Kerensky alone of the Petrograd Soviet representatives determined to join the government, portraying himself as the 'hostage of the democracy' within it. Thus was born 'dual power'. In spite of the prevailing mood of national unity, it reflected the deep division in Russian society between the 'democracy' and 'propertied society'.

Outside Petrograd dual power was much less in evidence. In most localities a broad alliance of social groups formed committees of public organizations to eject police and tsarist officials, maintain order and food supply, and to oversee the democratization of the town councils and zemstvos. The government endeavoured to enforce its authority by appointing commissars, most of whom were chairs of county zemstvos and thus representatives of landed or business interests. By summer the parallel existence of the committees, the commissars, the town councils and zemstvos – which by this stage were undergoing democratic election – and the soviets reflected the deep fragmentation of power in provincial towns and cities. In rural areas peasants expelled land captains, township elders, and village policemen and set up township committees under their control. The government attempted to strengthen its authority by setting up land and food committees at township level, but these too fell under peasant control. At the very lowest level the authority of the village gathering was strengthened by the revolution, although it became 'democratized' by the participation of younger sons, landless labourers, village intelligentsia (scribes, teachers, vets, and doctors), and some women. The February Revolution thus devolved power to the localities and substantially reduced the capacity of the Provisional Government to make its writ run beneath the county level.

Until autumn the popular organizations everywhere were dominated by the Mensheviks and SRs. The Mensheviks had originated as a faction of the RSDLP in 1903 after they objected to Lenin's model of a vanguard party, fearing that professional revolutionaries would substitute themselves for the working class. As orthodox Marxists, they believed that Russia did not yet have the prerequisites for socialism: a developed industry and a large working class. Because many – possibly most – RSDLP organizations in the provinces had declined to split along factional lines, it is difficult to estimate how many Mensheviks there were in 1917. By May, there were probably around 100,000 – half of them in Georgia – rising to nearly 200,000 by autumn. The SRs, led by

V. M. Chernov, were by far the largest party in 1917. They rejected the Marxist view of the peasantry as petty-bourgeois, believing that the principles of collectivism inherent in the peasant commune made Russia peculiarly fitted for socialism. For this reason, and because they put so much energy into organizing the peasantry during 1905–7, they were seen as the party of the peasantry. By autumn 1917, however, alongside 700,000 members in the army and in the villages, the SRs had 300,000 members in the towns, making them as significant an urban force as the Bolsheviks. The question of whether or not to support the tsarist government in the war had split both Mensheviks and SRs deeply. These internal splits deepened in the course of 1917, especially among the SRs. Their right wing called for war to victory; their centre faction, led by Chernov, shifted a long way from its principles in pursuit of the coalition with the bourgeoisie; while the left wing, who became the Left SRs, increasingly took up a programme that differed little from that of the Bolsheviks.

Despite the talk of 'unity of the vital forces of the nation', the issue of policy on the war put a great strain on the alliance between the Petrograd Soviet and the government. All sections of the populace hoped that the revolution would bring about a speedy peace and most of the moderate socialists on the Soviet executive had been opposed to the war hitherto. The Georgian Menshevik I. G. Tsereteli crafted a policy designed, on the one hand, to press the government to seek a comprehensive peace settlement, based on the renunciation of all annexations and indemnities, and on the other, to persuade soldiers that it was their duty to go on defending Russia until peace came about. The Provisional Government formally accepted this policy, but many of its members favoured war to victory. On 20 April, a note to the Allies from the Foreign Minister, P. N. Miliukov, leader of the Kadets, revealed his support for Allied war aims, as set out in secret treaties, which *inter alia* promised Russia the straits at the mouth of the Black Sea as the prize of victory. Immediately, outraged soldiers and workers took to the streets of Petrograd to demand Miliukov's resignation. Among them could be seen Bolshevik banners proclaiming 'Down with the Provisional Government'. On 2 May Miliukov was forced to resign and Prince Lvov insisted that members of the Soviet executive join a coalition government to resolve the crisis.

Having entered the government to speed the conclusion of peace, the six socialists who sat alongside eight 'bourgeois' ministers found themselves embroiled in preparations for war. Kerensky, the new War Minister, was determined to see the Russian army launch a new offensive out of a desire to see Russia honour her treaty obligations to the Allies. It was clear, however, that many units were reluctant to go on the attack. Kerensky toured the fronts frenetically, whipping up support. In the event only 48 battalions refused to go into action. The offensive quickly turned into a rout. Losses amounted to 400,000 men and the number of deserters was even greater. From now on indiscipline turned into organized disobedience, as the committees fell increasingly under the sway of principled opponents of the war such as Left SRs and Bolsheviks. In retrospect – although this was not evident at the time – this can be seen as the beginning of the end for the Provisional Government, since no government can long survive without control over the armed forces.

Until June the Bolsheviks remained on the margin of politics. On 3 April Lenin, the party's founder and undisputed leader, returned after almost 16 years in exile. He was a man of iron will and self-discipline, personally modest yet supremely self-confident and intolerant of opponents. His politics were rooted in Marxist theory, which he sought to adapt to Russian conditions, yet he had a capacity to make sharp adjustments to policy and to take tough decisions. Upon his return, his contempt for liberalism and parliamentarianism, his implacable opposition to the 'imperialist' war, and his appreciation of the mass appeal of soviets caused him to take up what appeared to be very extreme positions. In fact his extremism oriented him well towards the underlying realities of politics. L. B. Kamenev and I. V. Stalin, upon their return from Siberian

4. Russian soldiers demonstrating in Petrograd, April 1917

exile on 12 March, had committed the party to conditional support for the Provisional Government, a revolutionary defencist position on the war, and to negotiations with the Mensheviks to reunify the RSDLP. In his *April Theses* Lenin denounced each of these policies, insisting that there should be no support for the government of 'capitalists and landlords', that the character of the war had changed not one jot, and that the Bolsheviks should campaign for power to be transferred to the soviets. Crucially, Lenin concluded that the revolution was moving from its 'bourgeois' stage towards the socialist stage, the First World War having convinced him that capitalism was in its death throes and that socialism was now on the agenda internationally. Trotsky, who had clashed swords with Lenin on many occasions in his Menshevik past, welcomed this conversion to views closer to his own.

In 1917 the Bolshevik party was very different from the tightly knit conspiratorial party advocated by Lenin in 1903. Though more unified than the SRs, Mensheviks, and anarchists, the Bolsheviks were a diverse lot and even after Lenin's *April Theses* became official policy, the gradualist views of Kamenev and G. E. Zinoviev (dubbed 'Lenin's mad dog' by the Mensheviks) continued to enjoy strong support. Alongside cadres who had endured years of persecution, tens of thousands of workers, soldiers, and sailors flooded into the party, knowing little Marxism, but seeing in the Bolsheviks the most committed defenders of the working class. Bolsheviks were indefatigable in agitating for their policies in factories and on street corners. The result was that party membership rose from perhaps 10,000 in March to nearly 400,000 by October.

On the afternoon of 3 July, soldiers of the First Machine-Gun Regiment, angry at the failure of the June offensive and determined not to be sent to the front, took to the streets to demand that power be transferred to the soviets. Joined by 20,000 Kronstadt sailors and thousands of workers, they precipitated the severest crisis of the government to date, known as the July Days, a crisis compounded by the resignation of the

5. Troops firing on Bolsheviks in July demonstrations

Kadet ministers from the government. Rank-and-file Bolsheviks, including members of the party's Military Organization, were involved in calling the demonstration, but the Central Committee was alarmed at the initiative, since it did not believe that the time was ripe for the overthrow of the government. When the movement showed no sign of abating, however, it resolved to lead it. On 4 July a semi-insurrection got underway, as armed soldiers surrounded the headquarters of the government. However, the latter was able to bring in reliable military units and scattered the insurgents. Tsereteli anguished that 'it fell to me as Minister of Internal Affairs to apply repressive methods against those who in the past had been my comrades in the struggle for freedom.' Kerensky ordered 'severe retribution' against the Bolsheviks whom he branded 'German agents'. Orders were issued for the arrest of Lenin, Trotsky, and other leading Bolsheviks, causing Lenin to flee to Finland and the others to be jailed. It looked as though the Bolsheviks were a spent force. Kerensky delighted in his triumph.

The nationalist challenge

The 1897 census revealed that Russians comprised only 44% of the total population of the empire. The more accurate 1926 census recognized the existence of 194 different ethnic groups, varying enormously in size, language, religion, culture, and level of socio-economic development. Nationalist movements had first posed a challenge to the autocracy in 1905 and during the war many became radicalized as the peripheral regions of the empire experienced foreign occupation and evacuation, as Polish and Latvian regiments were formed within the tsarist army, and as Allied propaganda circulated about national self-determination as an Allied war aim. Nationalism, however, was extremely unevenly developed across the empire. Among the 18 million Muslims, for example, it was a weak force. Only the Tatars of the middle Volga, Urals, and Crimea, a scattered population interspersed with Russians, showed much political consciousness and they tended to support a pan-Islamic solution – i.e. extra-territorial, cultural autonomy for all Muslims within a unitary Russian state – rather than a nationalist solution based on each ethnic group having its own national territory. Among the biggest concentration of Muslims in Turkestan – a vast region, which ranged from the northern desert steppe (modern Kazakhstan) east to the khanates of Khiva and Kokand and the emirate of Bukhara, each based on oases and river agriculture – there was barely any ethnic awareness, identities being defined in terms of clans, villages, and oases or, at the macro-level, in terms of the commonwealth of Islam. By contrast, in the Baltic region, the dominance of Germans, together with periodic campaigns of Russification by the tsarist state, had stimulated rather strong nationalist movements, in spite of the fact that neither Latvia nor Estonia had any history of independent statehood.

The Provisional Government seriously underestimated the destabilizing power of nationalism in 1917, fondly imagining that the abrogation of discriminatory legislation would 'solve' the national question. After February, the most common nationalist demands were not for outright secession but for rights of cultural self-expression and for a measure of political autonomy within the framework of a federal Russian state. Typical was the slogan of the liberal and socialist politicians of the Ukrainian Rada, or National Council: 'Long Live Autonomous Ukraine in a Federated Russia'. Only in the untypical cases of Poland and Finland – where existing states had retained some autonomy after incorporation into the empire – did nationalists demand complete separation. By contrast, in the equally untypical cases of Armenia and Georgia, where nationalism was also strong – both countries having long histories as political entities and their own Christian churches – politicians tended to support the Provisional Government. In the case of the Armenians, who were dispersed between Russia, Turkey, and Persia, the genocide unleashed against them by Turks during the war led the moderate socialist party, known as Dashnaktsutiun, to support the Provisional Government out of fear of Turkey. In Georgia the nationalist movement was dominated by Mensheviks, who had forged a mass movement based on the working class and, unusually, on the peasantry. Naturally, they were close to the Provisional Government.

Among the non-Russian masses demands for radical social and economic policies generally eclipsed purely nationalist demands. In general, peasants preferred parties that spoke to them in their own tongue and defended local interests, but they would only support nationalists when they backed their own struggles against the landed gentry. In Ukraine, the nationalist movement was politically divided, weakened by pronounced regional divisions, and limited by the fact that nearly a quarter of the population, concentrated in the towns, was Russian, Jewish, or Polish. Nevertheless the socio-economic grievances of the peasantry had an ethnic dimension since most landowners were Russians or Poles. The middle-class politicians of the Rada were forced to take an increasingly radical stance on the land question in order to maintain peasant support. As this suggests, nationalism was strongest where it was underpinned by powerful class sentiment. In Latvia, for example, a large working class and lower middle class faced a commercial and industrial bourgeoisie that was Jewish, Russian, or Polish. In 1917 nationalist politicians of a liberal or moderate socialist hue rapidly lost ground to Latvian Social Democracy which had a base among workers and landless peasants, the latter hating the 'grey barons', or Latvian farmers, almost as much as the German nobility. Generally, workers in the non-Russian areas were more likely to respond to class politics than to nationalism. In the Donbas and the cities of eastern Ukraine, for example, there was a strong working class, but it comprised Russians and Russianized Ukrainians who supported the pan-Russian struggle for soviet power rather than a strictly nationalist agenda.

As 1917 wore on, nationalist politicians steadily stepped up their demands for autonomy, partly in the face of obduracy by the Provisional Government, partly as politics in general radicalized. In Estonia the government redrew administrative boundaries along ethnic lines after February but the elected assembly, known as Maapäev, was dissatisfied with the extent of autonomy on offer. Challenged from the left by Russian-dominated soviets, it steadily moved towards demanding complete autonomy. The reluctance of the government to concede meaningful autonomy was motivated partly by fear that nationalist movements were a Trojan horse for Germany, and by deep attachment to a unified Russian state, especially strong among the Kadets. This was particularly evident in relation to Ukraine. With approximately 22% of the empire's population, Ukraine was by far the largest minority area, and its resources of grain, coal, and iron, together with its strategic position, made it of paramount importance to the government. The latter resisted the Rada's demands for limited devolution of power, with the result that it moved steadily in the direction of separatism. When in September Kerensky finally endorsed the principle of self-determination 'but only on such principles as the Constituent Assembly shall determine', it was too little, too late, and in November the Rada declared Ukraine a republic.

Social polarization

At the root of the crisis that overtook the Provisional Government after July lay a serious deterioration of the economy. In the first half of 1917 production of fuel and raw materials fell by at least a third, with the result that many enterprises closed temporarily or permanently. By October, nearly half a million workers had been laid off. The crisis was aggravated by mounting chaos in the transport system, which led to a shortage of bread in the cities. Between July and October prices rose fourfold and the real value of wages plummeted. Between February and October 2.5 million workers went on strike mainly for higher wages, but though strikes increased in scale during the autumn, especially in the Central Industrial Region close to Moscow, they became ever harder to win outright.

> We demand that the Ministry of Labour speedily order the factory owners and industrialists to stop their game of 'cat and mouse' and immediately undertake the increased extraction of coal and ore and also the production of agricultural tools and equipment, so as to reduce the number of unemployed and halt the closure of factories. If Messrs Capitalists will not pay attention to our demand, then we, the workers of the iron-rolling shop, demand complete control of all branches of industry by the toiling people. Of you capitalists, weeping your crocodile tears, we demand that you stop crying about devastation that you yourselves have created. Your cards are on the table. Your game is up.
>
> Resolution of the general meeting of the iron-rolling shop of the Putilov works, August 1917

The factory committees responded to the crisis by implementing workers' control of production. Being the labour organizations closest to the rank-and-file, the committees were the first to register the shift in working-class sentiment away from the moderate socialists towards the Bolsheviks. The first conference of Petrograd factory committees at the end of May overwhelmingly passed a Bolshevik resolution on control of the economy. As the economy began to collapse, the factory committees mobilized to prevent what they saw as widespread 'sabotage' by the employers. Workers' control signified the close monitoring of the activities of management; it was not intended to displace management but to ensure that management did not lay off workers in order to maintain profits. Employers, however, resented any infringement of their 'right to manage' and class conflict flared up on a dramatic scale. In the Donbas and Urals employers abandoned the ailing mines and metallurgical plants, leaving the committees struggling to maintain production. The idea of workers' control had not emanated from any political party, but the willingness of Bolsheviks, anarchists, and Left SRs to support it was a major factor in their growing popularity. By contrast, the insistence of moderate socialists that workers' control merely exacerbated chaos in the economy turned workers against them.

In the countryside conflict also began to increase during the summer. The first signs of trouble came when peasants resisted government attempts to get them to hand over grain. The war had seen a fall in the volume of grain marketed – it fell from one-quarter of the harvest before 1914 to one-sixth by 1917 – since peasants had no incentive to sell grain when there were no goods to buy and when the currency was losing its value. Concerned to feed the army and the towns, the government introduced a state monopoly on the sale of grain, but its attempts to induce peasants to sell grain at fixed prices provoked antagonism, peasants preferring to conceal grain or turn it into moonshine. More ominously, peasants grew restive at the slow progress towards solving the land question. The government had set up an unwieldy structure of land committees to prepare the details of the reform, thereby heightening peasant expectations, but was loath to begin land redistribution while millions of soldiers were still in the field. In addition, it was torn between the Kadets, who insisted that landlords must be fully recompensed for land taken from them, and Chernov, the Minister of Agriculture, who wished to see the orderly transfer of gentry estates to the land committees. From early summer, peasants began to take the law into their own hands. They acted cautiously at first, unilaterally reducing or refusing to pay rents, grazing cattle illegally, stealing wood from the landlord's forests, and, increasingly, taking over uncultivated tracts of gentry land on the pretext that this would boost the nation's grain supply. In the non-black-earth zone, where dairy and livestock farming were paramount, peasants concentrated on getting their hands on meadowland and pasture. Because of the inability of local authorities to react, illegal acts soared, levelling off somewhat during the harvest, but climbing sharply again from September. By autumn peasants were seizing the land, equipment, and livestock on gentry estates and redistributing them outright, especially in Ukraine. As one peasant explained: 'The *muzhiki* (peasant men) are destroying the squires' nests so that the little bird will never return.'

By summer the discourse of democracy put into circulation by the February Revolution was being overtaken by a discourse of class, a shift symbolized by the increasing use of the word 'comrade' instead of 'citizen' as the favoured mode of address. Given the underdevelopment of class relations in Russia, and the key role played in politics by such non-class groups as soldiers and nationalist movements, this was a remarkable development. After all, the language of class, at least in its Marxist guise, had entered politics only after 1905; yet it had been disseminated through endless strikes, demonstrations, speeches, leaflets, newspapers, and labour organizations. The layer of 'conscious' workers, drawn mainly from the ranks of skilled, literate young men, served as the conduit through which ideas of class and socialism passed to the wider workforce. The discourse proved easily assimilable, since it played on a deeply rooted distinction in popular culture between 'them', the *verkhi*, those at the top, and 'us', the *nizy*, those at the bottom. In 1917 'we' could signify the working class, 'proletarian youth', 'working women', the 'toiling people', or 'revolutionary democracy'. 'They' could signify capitalists, landlords, army generals or, at its most basic, *burzhui* – anyone with education, an overbearing manner, soft hands, or spectacles. The antipathy shown towards such groups as engineers or rural schoolteachers testifies to how indiscriminate the rhetoric of class could become.

The discourse of class served to cement two contending power blocs and to articulate fundamentally opposed sets of values and visions of the social order. It was at the root of the process of political polarization that escalated from late summer. Doubtless the salience of this discourse was linked to the way in which the discourse of nation became appropriated by conservatives. Faced with what they perceived to be processes of elemental revolt and national disintegration, the Kadets appealed to the nation to cast aside class and sectional interest. Yet if the class and nation became sharply counterposed, the discourse of class was in part an attempt to contest the Kadet vision of the nation-under-siege and to redefine the meaning of the nation in terms of the toiling people, playing on the double sense of the Russian word *narod*, which means both 'common people' and 'nation'.

The fall of the Provisional Government

Kerensky became prime minister following the July Days, presenting himself as the 'man of destiny' summoned to 'save Russia'. His posturing merely masked his impotence. On 19 July, in a bid to halt the disintegration of the army, he appointed General L. G. Kornilov Supreme Commander-in-Chief. Kornilov agreed to take up the post on condition that there was no interference by soldiers' committees in operational orders and that the death penalty was extended from soldiers at the front – already agreed – to those at the rear. Kerensky hoped to use the reactionary general to bolster his image as a strong man and restore the frayed ties with the Kadets, many of whom were openly talking about the need for a military dictatorship to save Russia from 'anarchy'. Kerensky and Kornilov agreed on the need to establish 'firm government' – code for suppressing the Bolsheviks – and each hoped to use the other to achieve his more particular ends. On 26 August, however, Kerensky lashed out at Kornilov after he received what seemed to be an ultimatum demanding that military and civil authority be placed in the hands of a supreme commander. Accusing Kornilov of conspiring to overthrow the government – and historians dispute as to whether he actually was – he sent a telegram relieving him of his duties. When Kornilov ignored the telegram and ordered troops to advance on Petrograd, he appears to have moved into open rebellion. His attempted coup, however, was poorly planned and the clandestine

6. General Kornilov

counter-revolutionary organizations that had looked to him as their saviour failed to respond. In a humiliating bid to save his government, Kerensky was forced to turn to the very soviets he had been planning to bring to heel, since they alone could prevent Kornilov's troops reaching the capital.

Kornilov's rebellion dramatically demonstrated the danger posed by the 'counter-revolution' and starkly underlined the feebleness of the Kerensky regime. No one, however, could have predicted that its immediate consequence would be to allow the Bolsheviks to stage a dramatic recovery, following their defeat in the July Days. On 31 August the Petrograd Soviet passed the Bolshevik resolution 'On Power', and the Moscow soviets followed on 5 September. In the first half of that month, 80 soviets in large and medium towns backed the call for a transfer of power to the soviets, although no one was entirely sure what the slogan 'All Power to the Soviets' – which belonged just as much to anarchists, Left SRs, and Menshevik Internationalists as to the Bolsheviks – actually meant. Whilst in hiding Lenin had written his most utopian work, *State and Revolution*, outlining his vision of a 'commune state' in which the three pillars of the bourgeois state (the police, standing army, and the bureaucracy) would be smashed and in which parliamentary democracy would be replaced by direct democracy based on the soviets. It is unlikely that many, even in the Bolshevik party, understood the slogan in this way. For most workers it meant a break with the coalition with the 'bourgeoisie', represented by the Provisional Government, and the formation of an all-socialist government representing all parties in the Soviet CEC.

The Bolshevik slogans of 'Bread, Peace, and Land' and 'All Power to the Soviets' were now taken up with alacrity. The party's consistent opposition to the government of 'capitalists and landowners', its rejection of the 'imperialist' war, and its calls for land to the peasants, power to the soviets, and workers' control seemed to hundreds of thousands of workers and soldiers to offer a way forward. Seeing this happen from his hiding-place in Finland, Lenin became convinced that nationally as well as internationally the time was now ripe for the Bolsheviks to seize power in the name of the soviets. He blitzed the Central Committee with demands that it prepare an insurrection, even threatening to resign on 29 September. 'History will not forgive us if this opportunity to take power is missed.' The majority of the leadership was unenthusiastic, believing that it would be better to allow power to pass democratically to the soviets by waiting for the Second Congress of Soviets, scheduled to open on 20 October. Lenin returned in secret to Petrograd and on 10 October persuaded the Central Committee to commit itself to the overthrow of the Provisional Government. Significantly, no timetable was set. Zinoviev and Kamenev were bitterly opposed to the decision, believing that the conditions for socialist revolution did not yet exist and that an insurrection was likely to be crushed. Lenin, however, argued that only by seizing power would popular support for a soviet government be consolidated. As late as 16 October, the mood in the party was against an insurrection and the decision of Zinoviev and Kamenev to make public their opposition drove Lenin to paroxysms of fury. It fell to Trotsky to make the practical preparations, which he did, not by following Lenin's scheme to launch an offensive against the capital by sailors and soldiers of the northern front, but by associating the insurrection with the defence of the Petrograd garrison and the Soviet.

On 6 October the government announced that half the garrison were to be moved out of the city to defend it against the sweeping German advance. Interpreting this as an attempt to rid the capital of its most revolutionary elements, the Soviet on 9 October created the embryo of a Military Revolutionary Committee (MRC) to resist the transfer. This was the organization that Trotsky used to unseat the government. There would have been no possibility of obeying Lenin's injunction to seize power prior to the Second Congress had the moderate socialists on the Soviet CEC not postponed its opening from 20 to 25 October, evidently to allow Kerensky time to prepare a pre-emptive strike against

7. Red Guards in Ekaterinburg

the Bolsheviks. On 20 October when the government ordered the transfer of troops to commence, the MRC ordered units not to move without its permission. On the night of 23–4 October Kerensky gave Trotsky the pretext he was looking for when he ordered the Bolshevik printing press to be shut down, as a prelude to moving against the MRC. On 24 October military units, backed by armed bands of workers, known as Red Guards, took control of bridges, railway stations, and other strategic points. Kerensky fled, unable to muster troops to resist the insurgents. By the morning of 25 October, only the Winter Palace, the headquarters of the government, remained to be taken. That afternoon Lenin appeared for the first time in public since July, proclaiming to the Petrograd Soviet that the Provisional Government

Dear Kolia

Why have you not written? Are you busy, or is it for some political reason? It's hard to believe you haven't written for six months. What are you up to? How are grandma and your mother? Are they in good health? What's happening in Tambov? What news have you? Here nothing remarkable is happening at present. True, these Bolshevik days have caused me great anxiety. I've been sitting here in the telegraph office until three or four in the morning. The office is guarded by Cossacks. We're in the theatre of military operations and political life is registered much more strongly than in Tambov, as strongly as in the capitals. Please write. I'm waiting to hear from you. The situation here is complicated, but no matter, I'm calm. We have here in Smolensk the icon of the Blessed Virgin, so in the past all disasters have passed us by. We believe this will continue in the future.

Your uncle

Smolensk, 29 October 1917

had been overthrown. 'In Russia we must now set about building a proletarian socialist state.' At 10.40 p.m. the Second Congress of Soviets finally opened against the sound of distant artillery bombardment of the Winter Palace. The Mensheviks and SRs denounced the insurrection as a provocation to civil war and demonstratively walked out, Trotsky's taunt echoing in their ears: 'You are miserable bankrupts; your role is played out. Go where you ought to be: into the dustbin of history.'

The seizure of power is often presented as a conspiratorial coup against a democratic government. It had all the elements of a coup – albeit one much advertised in the press – except for the fact that a coup implies the seizure of a functioning state machine. Arguably, Russia had not had this since February. The reasons for the failure are not hard to pinpoint. Lacking legitimacy from the first, the Provisional Government relied on the moderate socialists in the Petrograd Soviet to make its writ felt. From the summer it was engulfed by a concatenation of crises – at the front, in the countryside, in industry, and in the non-Russian periphery. Few governments could have coped with such a situation, and certainly not without an army to rely on.

Many historians argue that democratic government was simply a non-starter in Russia in 1917. The analysis above leans to that conclusion but we should note that in spring there was widespread enthusiasm for 'democracy'. Workers, soldiers, and peasants showed enthusiasm for a constitution, a republic, and civil rights; yet such matters were always secondary to the solution of their pressing socio-economic problems. It was the soviets and the factory committees, the institutions dedicated to promoting the social revolution, that were perceived as truly democratic. In other words, from the first, a heavily 'socialized' conception of democracy vied with a liberal notion of democracy tied to the defence of private property. The fact that the bases for a democratic regime were slender does not mean that they were non-existent, not at least if we think in terms of a regime that was socialist rather than liberal in complexion. If the Petrograd Soviet, having taken power in March, had hastened to summon the Constituent Assembly and to tackle the land question, the SRs and Mensheviks might have been able to consolidate a parliamentary regime. Following the Kornilov rebellion, a majority of moderate socialists finally came round to the view that the coalition with the 'bourgeoisie' had to end, and took up demands for a speedy end to the war, the transfer of land to the land committees, and the immediate summoning of the Constituent Assembly. If these demands had been raised in the spring it might have made all the difference. But then again, there were many in the SR party whose instincts were little different from those of Kerensky and who would have insisted on continuing the war, at least pending an international peace conference (something the Allies had no intention of agreeing to). And therein lay the rub. For the fate of democracy in 1917 was ultimately sealed by the decision to continue the war. It was the war that focused the otherwise disparate grievances of the people. It was war that exacerbated the deep polarization in society to a murderous extent. In 1902 Karl Kautsky, the leader of the German Social Democrats, had warned:

> Revolution which arises from war is a sign of the weakness of the revolutionary class, and often the cause of further weakness, because of the sacrifice it brings with it, and because of the moral and intellectual degradation to which war gives rise.

In the last analysis, it was the war that made the Bolshevik seizure of power irresistible.

Chapter 2
Civil war and the foundation of the Bolshevik regime

The October seizure of power generated an exhilarating sense that a new world was in the offing where justice and equality would triumph over arbitrariness and exploitation, where the power of nature would be harnessed to ensure plenty for all. In the eyes of most workers and soldiers, as well as many peasants, a soviet government signalled land and freedom, the triumph of equality and justice, vengeance on the old privileged classes, and rule by the toilers. The Bolsheviks deprecated the charge that they were utopians, insisting that the seizure of power was in step with the logic of capitalist development. Yet like revolutionaries everywhere they could not have endured without an idealized vision of the future society. According to the constitution of July 1918, the aim was nothing less than the:

> abolition of all exploitation of man by man, the complete elimination of the division of society into classes, the ruthless suppression of the exploiters, the establishment of a socialist organization of society, and the victory of socialism in all countries.

Determined to project their radical difference from the temporizing Provisional Government, they issued no fewer than 116 different decrees up to 1 January 1918 – on the burning questions of peace, land, and workers' control, and on such varied matters as divorce, self-determination for the Armenians in Turkey, and reform of the alphabet.

In spite of their utopianism, the Bolsheviks were initially circumspect as to whether socialism was immediately on the cards, since they were well aware that none of the material preconditions for socialism existed in this torn and backward country. They hoped that revolution would break out in the more developed countries of Europe, by no means an idle hope given the devastation wrought by the First World War. In the course of 1918 the war did indeed bring about the demise of the German, Austro-Hungarian, and Ottoman empires, and the Bolsheviks were particularly excited by the prospect of a revolution in Germany, since it had a large industrial base and well-organized working class. A. A. Ioffe, Soviet representative in Berlin, spent over a million marks attempting to promote a Bolshevik-style revolution that would come to the assistance of Soviet Russia. But although the Kaiser was overthrown, following the armistice in November 1918, and although German soldiers and workers formed soviets, most of them came to the conclusion that the short-term benefits of reform outweighed the costs of revolution. Right up to 1923, however, Europe continued to be profoundly unsettled and Bolshevik hopes were regularly raised by uprisings in Germany, Italy, and the former Habsburg empire.

On 26 October 1917 the Soviet government called on the belligerent powers to begin peace negotiations on the basis of no annexations or indemnities and self-determination for national minorities. They also published the secret treaties of the Allies to expose the 'filthy machinations of imperialist diplomacy'. Not surprisingly, the Entente spurned the Peace Decree, leaving the Bolsheviks little option but to make a separate peace with Germany. The terms proposed by Germany were tough and the majority of the Central Committee refused to accept them. On 18 February 1918 the German High Command sent 700,000 troops into Russian territory meeting virtually no resistance. On 23 February they proffered terms that were even more draconian. At the Central Committee meeting that evening, Lenin insisted that the terms be accepted, gaining seven votes; Trotsky, who favoured doing nothing, gained four votes; and the left, who favoured a revolutionary war against Germany, gained four votes. The peace treaty was duly signed at Brest-Litovsk on 3 March 1918. It was massively punitive, excising from the former empire the Baltic provinces and a large part of Belorussia and Ukraine, depriving Russia of access to one-third of the former empire's agricultural land and railways, virtually all its oil and cotton, and three-quarters of its coal and iron.

> We must organize our lives according to new labour and socialist principles whereby exploitation by landlords and capitalists, division between masters and slaves no longer exists; whereby only labour and equality reign, whereby all rights, benefits, and wealth belong exclusively to the toilers. The strengthening of these new labour principles demands acceptance and implementation of emergency economic and other measures by the toiling people, starting with the village, then the market town, the township, county, province, region, and ending with the all-Russian centre. It demands the creation of a single toilers' government to guarantee speedily the gains of the toilers.
>
> Declaration of the Perm county soviet of peasant and worker deputies,
> 14 March 1918

The other major decree issued by the Bolsheviks was that on land, which legitimized the spontaneous seizure of lands owned by the landed gentry, church, and crown and their transfer into peasant hands. Significantly, it did not embody the party's policy of nationalization – taking land into state ownership – but the SR policy of socialization: 'land passes into the use of the entire toiling people'. This left communes free to decide how they would apportion land. It was a hugely popular measure. In the central black-earth provinces three-quarters of landowners' land was confiscated between November 1917 and January 1918. How much better off peasants were as a result, is hard to say, since there was no uniformity in the amount of land peasants received even within a single township, not to speak of the many regions where there were no gentry estates to redistribute. Nation-wide the average allotment expanded by about an acre, but this masks substantial variation. Slightly over a half of all communes received no additional land, and since two-thirds of the land confiscated was already farmed by peasants, the amount of new land that passed into the hands of the peasants only represented just over a fifth of the entire cultivated area. In addition, however, the situation of the peasants was improved by the abolition of rents and loan repayments. Overall, the principal result of the land redistribution was to reduce the extent of social differentiation among the peasantry, reducing the number of wealthy and very poor households and strengthening the ranks of the middling smallholders. Of great concern to the government was the fact that in Russia and Ukraine the most commercialized and technically sophisticated estates and farms were broken up, thereby exacerbating the already lamentable productivity of agriculture.

The widespread expectation was that the Bolshevik seizure of power would lead to the establishment of a government representing all the parties in the Soviet CEC, pending the convening of a Constituent Assembly. On 26 October 1917, however, Lenin formed a Council of People's Commissars, known as Sovnarkom, all 15 members of which were Bolsheviks. Talks to form a coalition got underway, but were scuttled by the intransigence of hard-liners on all sides. Five Bolsheviks promptly resigned from Sovnarkom on the grounds that 'we consider a purely Bolshevik government has no choice but to maintain itself by political terror.' On 10 December, however, the Left SRs, who had now finally split from the main party, agreed to accept seven posts in the government on condition that Sovnarkom became accountable to the CEC. It was they who helped craft the law on land redistribution and engineered the fusion of the All-Russian Soviet of Peasant Deputies, whose SR-dominated executive had backed military resistance to the Bolsheviks, with the CEC.

Prior to October the Bolsheviks had made much political capital out of the decision by the Provisional Government to postpone elections to the Constituent Assembly from September to November, since the Constituent Assembly symbolized the people's power at the heart of the revolution. Having seized power, however, it was by no means clear that the Bolsheviks would get a majority in the Assembly. Lenin believed that soviet power, being based on direct election by the toilers, was superior to parliamentary democracy, since parliaments merely served to camouflage control of the state machine by the capitalist class. The Bolsheviks nevertheless decided that the elections should go ahead. According to the latest research, 48.4 million valid votes were cast, of which the SRs gained 19.1 million, the Bolsheviks 10.9 million, the Kadets 2.2 million, and the Mensheviks 1.5 million. The non-Russian socialist parties – mostly sympathetic to the SRs – received over 7 million, including two-thirds of votes in Ukraine. The SRs were thus the clear winners, their vote concentrated in the countryside. The Bolsheviks received the majority of worker votes, together with 42% of the 5.5 million soldiers' votes, but it was clear that they could not hope to have a majority in the Assembly. This vote, incidentally, represented the peak of popular support for the party. Hereafter they lost support as soldiers returned to their villages and as worker disaffection grew.

The Constituent Assembly opened in dispiriting circumstances on 5 January, shortly after pro-assembly demonstrators had been gunned down by Red Guards. The Bolsheviks insisted that the delegates accept soviet power as a *fait accompli*, but the delegates chose to discuss the agenda proposed by the SRs, making Chernov the chair of the Assembly. After a single session, Bolshevik soldiers shut the Assembly down. It is not beyond the realm of possibility that a deal could have been struck. Some 85% of the delegates were socialists – the 200 SR delegates had spent a total of 1,000 years in prison and hard labour – and on the crucial issues of peace and land, the SRs had shifted closer to the Bolshevik position. But the delegates were not prepared to give way on what was for the Bolsheviks the crucial issue: the abandonment of parliamentary democracy in favour of a 'dictatorship of the proletariat', based on the soviets. By closing the Constituent Assembly the Bolsheviks signalled that they were ready to wage war in defence of their regime not only against the exploiting classes, but against the socialist camp. The dissolution doomed the chances of democracy in Russia for 70 years; for that the Bolsheviks bear the largest share of the blame. Yet the prospects for a democratic socialist regime had by this stage become extremely slender. It is true that some 70% of the peasants voted in the Assembly elections – including more women than men – but they did so less out of enthusiasm for democratic politics than out of a desire to see the Assembly legalize their title to the land. Once it became clear that they had no reason to fear on that score, they acquiesced in the Assembly's dissolution, testifying to the thinness of a culture of democracy and law.

Soviet power was established with surprising ease – a reflection of the popularity of the idea of devolving power to the toilers. Bolshevik support was strongest in towns and regions with a relatively homogeneous working class, such as in the Central Industrial Region or the mining settlements of the Urals. In less industrial cities, such as Moscow and those along the Volga, the Bolsheviks often relied on the local garrison to declare soviet power; and in the capitals of the predominantly agrarian provinces and in smaller towns the Bolsheviks had difficulty ousting the SRs and Mensheviks from positions of control in the soviets. In Siberia the revolution was carried along the Trans-Siberian railway and soviet power was declared everywhere by the beginning of 1918: support for the Bolsheviks was strong, in spite of the fact that workers and poor peasants, normally their strongest supporters, were few. In the countryside, peasant reactions were initially mixed. In the middle-Volga province of Saratov in November, 19 townships were favourable to soviet power, two were wavering, eight were unfriendly, and eight downright hostile. By February, however, 86% of townships had created soviets as an alternative to the zemstvos that were generally under SR control. In the central black-earth belt, progress was somewhat slower, with 83% of townships creating soviets between January and March. These local soviets believed they had complete control of their localities and ignored decrees of the centre with impunity. G. I. Petrovsky, Commissar of Internal Affairs, complained: 'They prefer their local interests to state interests, continuing to confiscate fuel, timber, designated for railways and factories.'

As early as spring 1918 there was a backlash against the Bolsheviks in many soviets in provincial towns. This was sometimes due, as in Kaluga or Briansk, to the demobilization of the local garrison and sometimes, as in Tver' or Iaroslavl', to the rapid growth of unemployment and the deterioration of the food supply. The arbitrary way in which the Bolsheviks dealt with opposition from soviets – manipulating their structure or closing down the more recalcitrant ones – added to their unpopularity. Yet the revival in the fortunes of the Mensheviks and the SRs should not be exaggerated. New elections to the Moscow Soviet from 28 March to 10 April, although marred by malpractice, gave them only a quarter of the vote. And even where their record was more impressive, the division between the two parties meant they were seldom able to mount an effective challenge to the Bolsheviks. Sometimes, moreover, the challenge came from the left, as in Samara where SR Maximalists declared a commune and ejected Red Guards. On 15 June, discarding the pretence that the soviets were multi-party bodies, the Bolsheviks expelled Mensheviks and SRs from the CEC. This proved to be a decisive step in the subordination of the CEC to Sovnarkom. On 29 May a party circular spelt out the logic of the situation: 'Our party stands at the head of soviet power. Decrees and measures of soviet power emanate from our party.'

Civil war

The years between 1918 and 1922 witnessed a level of strife and anarchy unparalleled since the 'Time of Troubles' of 1605–13, when struggles between pretenders to the throne brought Russia to a state of chaos.

The civil war brutalized social life to an unimaginable degree, yet as an epic struggle between the new and old worlds it inspired idealism and heroism among the dedicated minorities who supported the Red and White causes. The young Bolshevik, V. Poliansky, recalled:

> We all lived in an atmosphere of revolutionary romanticism, tired, exhausted, but joyful, festive, our hair uncut, unwashed, unshaven, but bright and clear in heart and mind.

Yet the reality was that Russia succumbed to an economic and social cataclysm. The population on Soviet territory fell by 12.7 million between 1917 and early 1922, only partly due to civil war as such. The losses of Soviet armed forces ranged from 1,150,000 to 1,250,000; and when the losses of Whites, partisans and nationalist forces are included, war-related losses rise to between 2.5 million and 3.3 million. Far more perished as a result of disease – between 1917 and 1920 over 2 million died of typhus, typhoid fever, smallpox, and dysentery – causing Lenin to warn that, 'either the louse will defeat socialism or socialism will defeat the louse.' Finally, and most hideously, between 1921 and 1922 as many as 6 million died of starvation and disease in a famine that devastated the Volga region and Ukraine. Not without reason did the novelist Boris Pasternak conclude: 'In our days even the air smells of death.' Meanwhile the brutalization that had begun with the First World War continued apace. Large quantities of weapons were now in the hands of ordinary people and civil authority was too weak to stanch the flow of violence. After his forces swept the Reds from the northern Caucasus in January 1919, General P. N. Wrangel recollected:

> On the outskirts of one of the Cossack settlements we met five young Cossacks with rifles . . . 'Where are you going, lads?' 'We're going to beat up some Bolsheviks. There are a lot of them hiding in the reeds. Yesterday I killed seven.' This was said by a boy about 12 years old. During the whole of the intestinal conflict I never felt as sharply as I did at that moment the utter horror of fratricidal war.

The civil war was dominated by the conflict between the Bolsheviks and the conservative nationalist officers who formed the various White armies, notably the Volunteer Army of General A. I. Denikin, the Siberian forces of Admiral A. V. Kolchak, and the Northwestern Army of General N. N. Iudenich. Yet the civil war was more than a straight struggle between Reds and Whites. Initially, the so-called 'democratic counter-revolution', led by the SRs, posed at least as great a threat to Bolshevik rule. More crucially, the struggle between Reds and Whites was played out in a context in which the Russian empire was disintegrating, and nationalist movements in Ukraine in 1918, in Ukraine, Estonia, Latvia, Lithuania, and Finland in 1919, and in Poland, Azerbaijan, and Armenia in 1920, made things more complicated for Reds and Whites alike. Furthermore, the civil war had international ramifications, initially in relation to the outcome of the First World War, later in relation to the carving out of post-war spheres of influence. The Allies intervened on the side of the Whites and this was an important, if not ultimately decisive factor in the conflict. Finally, the conflict between Reds and Whites became embroiled with powerful partisan movements, notably the Revolutionary Insurgent Army of Ukraine led by the anarchist N. Makhno, guerrilla actions by deserters, and innumerable peasant uprisings.

It is sensible to see the civil war building up gradually, beginning as early as the Kornilov movement and significantly escalating after the Bolshevik seizure of power. Soviet forces invaded independent Ukraine in December 1917 and by February had succeeded in forcing the nascent Volunteer Army, which struggled to establish a base among the Cossacks of the Don and Kuban regions, to retreat. In these early skirmishes, the Red Guards, Latvian riflemen, and other soviet forces proved to be an eager but ill-disciplined force; so it fell to Trotsky, as Commissar of War, to build a conventional army. In this he faced bitter resistance from those who believed that the only defence force appropriate to a socialist society was a citizens' militia. When only 360,000 men volunteered for the new Red Army, Trotsky on 29 May

1918 reinstated conscription. Vigorous measures were taken to enforce discipline among the largely peasant conscripts, including summary execution and the decimation of units. His most contentious decision was to put former tsarist officers – 'military specialists' – in operational command subject to the oversight of political-military commissars. To deter them from treason or desertion – few having much sympathy with the Red cause – their families were held hostage for their good behaviour. Trotsky proved to be an inspirational figure as he toured the front in his famous headquarters train; but he was not infallible as a military commander and his authoritarian methods alienated many. This led to the formation of a Military Opposition, of which Stalin was a supporter, that opposed the ruthless centralization of the Red Army at the Eighth Party Congress in March 1919.

An undreamed-of opportunity for the 'democratic counter-revolution' presented itself in May 1918 when the Czech Legion, a body of 38,000 men recruited by the tsarist government from Austro-Hungarian prisoners-of-war, revolted against the Bolsheviks. From this time on, one may speak of full-scale civil war, since armies now fought along clearly defined fronts. Within a few months, the Legion seized control of a vast area east of the Volga and helped the SRs to set up governments committed to overthrowing the Bolsheviks, restoring the Constituent Assembly, and resuming war with Germany. The revolt threw the Bolsheviks into panic. Secret orders were given by Lenin to execute the imperial family in Ekaterinburg lest they be liberated by the insurgents. In fact the SRs proved unable to translate the electoral support they had received in the Constituent Assembly into solid political support and, crucially, into forging a reliable army. Where they remained respectful of democracy and law they were ineffective; where they sought to be firm, they slid into habits not very different from those of the Reds and Whites. Having gone to considerable lengths to secure the cooperation of conservative military men, they ended up in hock to them, compromising what were for the peasants the most important gains of the revolution: land and the devolution of power to the localities. The

8. Trotsky reviewing the Red troops during the civil war, 1917

fate of SR attempts to create a 'third way' between the dictatorships of right and left was sealed on 18 November 1918 when Cossack officers arrested the SR members of the Omsk Directory and proclaimed Admiral Kolchak 'Supreme Ruler'.

Henceforward the civil war resolved into a conflict between Reds and Whites. The Whites stood for 'Russia, One and Indivisible', the restoration of state-mindedness, law and order, and the values of Orthodox Christianity. They strove to redeem the profaned honour of Russia's armed forces and presented themselves as being 'above class' and 'above party'. In fact, they were not a class movement in any strict sense, since they were slow to develop programmes that could have assisted landowners and industrialists to regain their property and power. So far as the political regime for which they were struggling was concerned, there was little unanimity concerning the shape it should take. Some such as General Wrangel of the Volunteer Army were committed monarchists; but most favoured some type of military dictatorship, possibly paving the way for a new Constituent Assembly. In an effort to keep political differences at bay, the Whites advanced the principle of 'non-predetermination', i.e. the postponement of all policy-making until the war was over. What kept them united in the meantime was little more than detestation of the Bolsheviks and outrage at the 'German-Jewish' conspiracy inflicted on the Russian people.

After a gruelling conflict, it was clear by spring 1920 that it was only a matter of time before the Reds triumphed. Historians differ in their assessment as to why the Reds won: some emphasize the weakness of the Whites; others insist that the Reds had positive advantages, but differ as to whether these were exclusively military in nature or political as well as military. If one compares the armies of the Reds and Whites, it becomes clear that the Reds had certain military advantages. Their army was larger: by autumn 1920 it had grown to over 5 million – although there were never more than half-a-million troops in the front line – compared with a combined total of 2 million White troops by spring 1920. Moreover, although the quality of both armies was evenly matched – both, for example, suffered from massive levels of desertion – the Reds had the edge so far as leadership was concerned. The Volunteer Army was formed around a core of 4,000 experienced officers; but this ceased to be an advantage once the Reds compelled 'military specialists' to enlist; and over time, the Reds proved able to nurture officers of talent such as V. K. Bliukher and M. N. Tukhachevsky. In addition, the Whites were riven by personal animosity, principally between Denikin and Kolchak and Denikin and Wrangel; the conflict between Trotsky and Stalin proved less damaging since the Bolsheviks had a binding ideology and a recognized leader. Finally, the Bolsheviks were clearly superior in the organizational sphere. The Red Army had a unified centre of command in the Revolutionary Military Council of the Republic, and was supported by such institutions as the Defence

9. Baron Wrangel leaves Russia

Council, which fused the civilian and defence sectors, the Cheka, and an underground party network in White-occupied areas.

Perhaps the greatest advantage enjoyed by the Reds was strategic: their possession of a centrally located and compact territory. This meant that they could send forces from one front to another without great difficulty since railways radiated outwards from Moscow. By contrast, the Whites were strung out along the periphery of European Russia. The Don base of the Volunteer Army was nearly 1,000 kilometres from Moscow; Kolchak's base in Omsk was almost 3,000 kilometres from Petrograd. Any advance into the heartland of soviet power created a problem of long supply lines and communication difficulties. Moreover, the possession by the Reds of the core territory, where the majority of the population and resources were concentrated, gave them control of key industrial centres as well the stocks of the tsarist army. The Whites, by contrast, had control of only secondary centres of the defence industry in the Donbas and Urals, although they were better supplied with coal. As against that, they had an abundance of food, especially in Siberia and the Kuban region, so soldiers in the White armies were generally better fed than their Red counterparts, whose ration norm of 410 grams of bread per day was lower than in the tsarist army.

Some see the military advantages of the Reds as overwhelming, but that is to make too much of hindsight. A military victory for the Whites was by no means an impossibility: if Kolchak and Denikin had advanced on Moscow simultaneously in 1919, rather than five months apart, or if Kolchak had struck a deal with the Finnish general Mannerheim (both of which were on the cards), the Red Army might well have gone under.

If military and strategic factors are paramount in explaining the White defeat, socio-political factors cannot be ignored. By 1919 all the White administrations recognized that they could not simply shelve the thorny issues of land reform, national autonomy, labour policy, and local government. The policies they concocted, however, offered too little, too late and exposed deep division in White ranks. First, with regard to the land, all White administrations accepted that there could be no return to the status quo ante, yet there were enough cases of officers returning former landowners to their estates to fix in peasant minds the notion that a White victory would bring about the return of the landlords. Whenever the Whites threatened, therefore, peasants swung behind the Reds. Second, the Whites had to deal with non-Russian nationalities; yet their hatred of what Denikin called the 'sweet poisonous dreams of independence' prevented them from making serious concessions. They would not recognize the independence of Finland and the Baltic states; they would not negotiate with J. Pilsudski, President of Poland from November 1918; they would not recognize a 'separatist' Ukrainian state. By contrast, the Bolsheviks, however much they alienated nationalists at times, were willing to grant a measure of self-government. Finally, despite trumpeting their devotion to the Russian people, the Whites failed to forge a concept of the nation with which peasants and workers could identify. With the Church on their side, they might have tried to play on the Orthodox faith of the majority, yet they proved too hidebound by a militaristic and narrowly elitist ethos to adapt to the world of mass politics. Ironically, it was the internationalist Bolsheviks who tapped into patriotic sentiment, exploiting the Whites' dependence on the Allies to portray them as playthings of foreign capital.

By the end of the civil war the Red Army had become the largest institution of state, enjoying absolute priority in the allocation of resources. In the absence of a numerous or politically reliable proletariat, it became by default the principal social base of the regime. Fighting to defend the socialist motherland, living in collective units, subject to political education, the army proved to be the seeding ground for the cadres who came to staff the apparatus of the party-state in the 1920s. It also proved to be the agency through which the revolution was brought to new areas. Instead of socialism being spread through mobilizing workers, the Bolsheviks came to believe that what

N. I. Bukharin called 'red intervention' was the best means of furthering socialism. In 1920, without the least embarrassment, the leading Bolshevik, K. B. Radek, could claim: 'We were always for revolutionary war. The bayonet is an essential necessity for introducing communism.'

Nationalism and empire

By October 1917 it looked as though the Russian empire might break up, in the way the Austro-Hungarian and Ottoman empires did, so it was important that the Bolsheviks should have a clear policy on the question of self-determination for the non-Russian peoples. In fact, they were divided on the matter. Lenin was sensitive to the oppression that the non-Russian peoples had experienced under tsarism and believed that they must be given the right to secede from the empire if there was to be any chance of them cooperating with the Russian proletariat in the longer term. The majority did not share his view. In December 1917 the new Commissar of Nationalities, Stalin, expressed the consensus view when he argued that self-determination should be exercised only by the labouring classes, and not by the bourgeoisie. Because they had no firm position, therefore, Bolshevik policy was determined to a large extent by pragmatic considerations.

On 31 December 1917 the Bolsheviks recognized the independence of Finland, something the Provisional Government had been reluctant to do. In the Baltic as a whole, however, they fought movements for national independence since support for soviet power was strong. In Latvia German occupation undermined the soviets and paved the way for a nationalist government. In Estonia, where soviets ran many towns, Bolshevik indifference to nationalist sensitivities, combined with failure to expropriate the German barons, strengthened support for the Maapäev which repelled the Red Army in early 1919, with assistance from Whites, the British, and Finnish volunteers. By 1920 the Bolsheviks were reconciled to the loss of Estonia and Latvia. In Belorussia and

Lithuania nationalism was weak and the defeat of Germany left a power vacuum which Poles and Reds sought to fill. After the Germans withdrew, the feeble government in Belorussia collapsed, allowing the Reds to take over. In March 1919 they merged Belorussia with Lithuania to form the Litbel soviet republic. The following month, however, Poland occupied Vilnius, the putative capital of independent Lithuania, reinstated landowners, and made Polish the official language. Nationalism was weak in Lithuania, the population being largely peasant and the small urban population Jewish or Polish, yet nationalists rather adeptly exploited the Soviet–Polish war to gain independence albeit within much reduced borders. By the Treaty of Riga, the Bolsheviks recognized the independence of the Baltic states and of a Poland whose eastern border extended well into Belorussian and Ukrainian-majority territory. Signed in March 1921, the treaty reflected the inability of either Russia or Poland to establish their hegemony in the Baltic in the way that Germany once had.

The loss of Ukraine was something the Bolsheviks found much harder to contemplate. No fewer than nine governments came and went in the space of three years, testifying to the inability of nationalists, Whites, or Reds to enforce control. Caught between the Reds and Whites, the intermittent nationalist governments turned for protection first to Germany, then to the Entente, and finally to Poland. Torn by political division, they found themselves increasingly at odds with a peasantry that looked for protection to the guerrilla bands of Makhno and the other *otomany*, or chiefs. The civil war devastated Ukraine but had a paradoxical effect on social identities. Ukrainian peasants turned inwards as centralized power broke down, yet their identification with the Ukrainian nation was strengthened as a result of independent statehood. Twice the Bolsheviks gained control of Ukraine and each time their promise of self-determination proved hollow. Only in 1920 after Moscow cleared Russian chauvinists out of leadership of the Ukrainian Communist Party did the new Soviet administration seriously address aspirations for self-determination. And in a pattern replicated elsewhere, radical nationalists, recognizing that they must settle for less than they would ideally like, accepted the Ukrainian Soviet Socialist Republic as a framework in which they could work.

Aspirations for Transcaucasian unity proved transient once the Russian army withdrew from the region in winter 1917–18. As Russian power receded, so Turkish influence increased, exacerbating ethnic tension, especially between Armenians and Azerbaijanis in Baku. In May this led to the collapse of the Transcaucasian Sejm and the emergence of three separate states, all of which were beset by fearsome economic difficulties, predation by the big powers, and mutual conflict over territorial boundaries. In Azerbaijan Musavat nationalists enjoyed little backing from the peasantry and support for soviet power remained strong in Baku. Falling oil revenues led to high unemployment and rocketing inflation. Independent Armenia, confined to a small landlocked territory around Erevan contested by its neighbours, was in an even more wretched state, inundated by refugees and wracked by starvation and disease. The Dashnaktsutiun formed a government of national emergency that quickly dropped any pretension to socialism. In Georgia, by far the most viable of the three states, the Mensheviks won 80% of the popular vote in 1919. Despite the economic chaos, they carried out land reforms and allowed trade unions and cooperatives to operate freely. The one blot on their record was the brutal treatment of ethnic minorities within Georgia.

Because of its petroleum and mineral resources, the Bolsheviks were determined to regain control of Transcaucasia. In April 1920 the Red Army invaded Azerbaijan and in September Armenia turned to it for help after it became embroiled in war with Turkey. By this stage, many nationalists in both countries saw in their own soviet republics the only viable form of statehood. In Georgia, however, this was not true. In May 1920 Moscow recognized Georgia against the wishes of Georgian communists such as S. Orjonikidze, one of Stalin's most loyal supporters. Yet in January 1921, in contravention of Moscow's orders

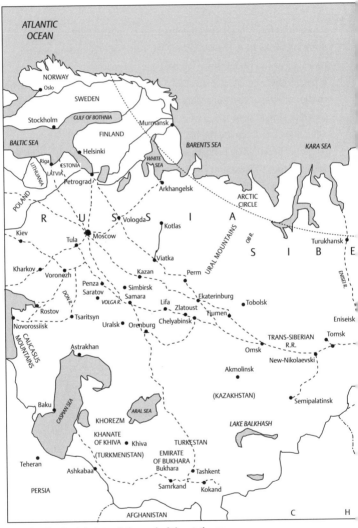

Map 2. The Soviet state at the end of the civil war

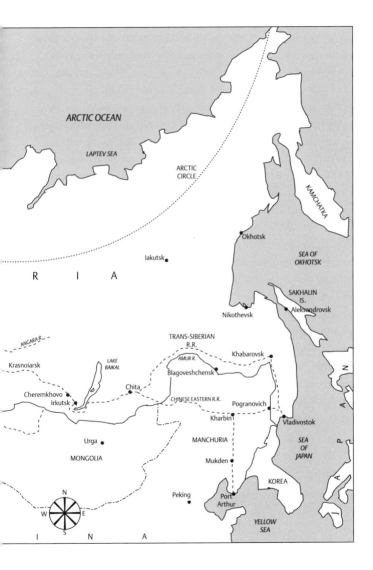

'not to self-determine Georgia', the Red Army marched in to the country.

On 24 November the Bolsheviks invited Muslims to order their national life 'freely and without hindrance', yet soviet power was everywhere established by ethnic Russians with a classically colonialist attitude towards the Muslim people. The claim of Tatar merchants, mullahs, and intellectuals to represent the community of Islam was widely resented by Muslims, not least by the Bashkirs of the southern Urals who, though closely related, were patronized by them for having given up nomadism relatively late. Radical Tatars, such as M. S. Sultangaliev, in the absence of a sizeable proletariat, seized on the creation of a Muslim Red Army as a vehicle to establish a Tatar-Bashkir state stretching from the mid-Volga to the Urals. Initially, Bashkirs sought to realize their aspirations by turning to the Whites, but it was not long before reform-minded Muslims and political radicals turned to the communists. Fearful of becoming junior partners in a Tatar-Bashkir state, they insisted on and got their own autonomous soviet socialist republic (ASSR) in March 1919. As early as June 1920, however, some began to defect to the guerrilla movement, known as the *basmachi*, in disgust at interference in their affairs by Russian communists on the ground. In Crimea, too, the left wing of the nationalist Milli Firka joined the communists; and once the Cheka had extirpated all opposition, a Crimean ASSR was proclaimed in October 1921. Meanwhile in the middle Volga a Tatar ASSR was finally established in May 1920, but it left 75% of the scattered Tatars outside its borders. Sultangaliev and his allies, who formed the core of the Tatarstan Communist Party, for a brief period brilliantly used the opportunity of having their own state to promote national identity among the Tatars.

In Turkestan there was still little agreement as to whether nationhood should be realized on an all-Turkestan scale or whether its constituent peoples should form separate states. In the steppes, the Alash Orda proclaimed Kazakh autonomy in December 1917 and turned to the

Whites in the face of the Red Army advance. By spring 1919, however, Kolchak's hostility to Kazakh autonomy swung it towards a compromise with the Bolsheviks. In August 1920 the Kazakhs received a polity of their own in the shape of an ASSR, clan and village structures being reconfigured into soviets. In Tashkent the Turkestan Council of People's Commissars refused to recognize the Kokand autonomous government, dominated as it was by reform-minded Muslims and conservative clerics. In February 1918 it carried out an appalling massacre, putting Kokand to the torch and slaughtering almost 60% of its inhabitants. Moscow stepped in to curb these excesses and ensured that ten Muslims were given positions in a new Turkestan Republic. This new government, however, managed to alienate the native population by seizing clerically held lands, closing religious schools, and abolishing *shariat* courts, so that by 1919 over 20,000 had joined the guerrillas. Following the capture of Bukhara in September 1920, the guerrilla movement spread to the whole of Central Asia, acquiring a pronounced Islamist character. It was not finally put down until 1925. The people's republics of Khorezm and Bukhara – their pre-industrial economies precluded their being called 'socialist' – along with the Turkestan ASSR lasted until 1924, when separate Uzbek, Turkmen, Tadzhik, and Kazakh republics were formed.

Overall, the civil war strengthened national identities yet deepened divisions within nationalist movements. Most nationalists proved unable politically or militarily to remain neutral in the contest between Reds and Whites and many ended up in hock to Germany, Turkey, Allied interventionists, or Poland. Most lacked solid popular support (there were exceptions, such as Georgia) and most fell prey to damaging conflicts over social and economic policies, especially concerning the land. By the end of the civil war, the Bolsheviks offered nationalists less than many wanted – although it is worth remembering that in 1917 few had aspired to complete national independence – yet far more than was on offer from Whites, the Allies, the Germans, or Turks. At the same time, they exploited the weakness of nationalism to reintegrate the bulk of the non-Russian territories into the Soviet Union. By 1922 the territory of the Soviet state was only 4% smaller than that of the tsarist empire. Moreover, the logic of this reincorporation was determined by many of the same geopolitical, security, and economic considerations that had governed the expansion of the tsarist state. A colossal territory unbroken by well-defined geographical or ethnic features, the unfavourable location of mineral resources, and above all, competition with rival states encouraged the reconstitution of a centralized quasi-imperial state. This did not mean that the Bolsheviks were simply old-style imperialists whose commitment to national self-determination was fraudulent. Despite the rampant racism of certain Bolsheviks on the ground, and the fact that the centre was never unequivocally in favour of granting national autonomy, policy in this period was generally animated by internationalism. It is not possible otherwise to explain why so much energy went into forging alliances with national movements or devising political frameworks for self-determination. Prior to 1917 the Bolsheviks had opposed the concept of federalism, preferring 'regional autonomy' within a unitary state. Yet, haphazardly, in response to forces that defied their control, they proceeded to restructure the former empire as a federation of soviet republics constituted along ethno-national lines. A form of federalism that gave non-Russian peoples a measure of political autonomy plus broad rights of cultural self-expression seemed to be the best means of reconciling the centrifugal impulses of nationalism with the centralizing impulse of the dictatorship of the proletariat.

Party dictatorship

In December 1917 the Cheka was set up to 'liquidate all attempts and acts of counter-revolution and sabotage'. It quickly turned into one of the most powerful organs of state, involved not only in eliminating counter-revolutionaries – of whom there were not a few – but also in combating speculation, corruption, and crime. By autumn 1918 the Cheka was associated above all with the Red terror. The Bolsheviks initially insisted that terror was a legitimate method of defending the dictatorship of the proletariat, but they promised to use it only as a last resort. As early as January 1918, however, Lenin warned: 'Until we use terror against speculators – shooting them on the spot – nothing will happen,' prompting the Left SR, I. N. Steinberg, to ask why in that case he should waste his time serving as Commissar of Justice. It was only with the near-fatal attack on Lenin by the anarchist F. Kaplan on 30 August 1918 that terror became elevated to official policy. In Petrograd the leading newspaper shrieked: 'For the blood of Lenin . . . let there be floods of blood of the bourgeoisie – more blood, as much as possible.'

My words to you, you bloodthirsty beast. You intruded into the ranks of the revolution and did not allow the Constituent Assembly to meet. You said: 'Down with prisons, Down with shootings, Down with soldiering. Let wage workers be secure.' In a word you promised heaps of gold and a heavenly existence. The people felt the revolution, began to breathe easily. We were allowed to meet, to say what we liked, fearing nothing. And then you, Bloodsucker, appeared and took away freedom from the people. Instead of turning prisons into schools, they're full of innocent victims. Instead of forbidding shootings, you've organized a terror and thousands of the people are shot mercilessly every day; you've brought industry to a halt so that workers are starving, the people are without shoes or clothes.

Letter from a Red Army soldier to Lenin, 25 December 1918

Between 1918 and February 1922, it has been estimated that 280,000 were killed by the Cheka and Internal Security Troops, about half in the course of operations to mop up peasant insurgents. This suggests that perhaps 140,000 were executed directly by the Cheka – a bloodcurdling number to be sure, but one that should be seen in the context of the 600,000 British and French troops who were sacrificed on the Somme in 1916 in order to advance seven miles. The Red terror was both spectacular – designed to strike terror into the hearts of the populace – and 'bureaucratic' in character. According to Cheka statistics, 128,010 were arrested in the RSFSR (All-Russian Socialist Federal Soviet Republic) in 1918–19, of whom 42% were released; of the rest who were tried, nearly 8% were shot and the rest incarcerated or sentenced to hard labour. By contrast, the White terror, which has received far less attention, was usually carried out when officers allowed their men to go on the rampage. In Ukraine at least 100,000 Jews perished at the hands of unruly soldiers of Denikin and the Ukrainian nationalist, S. V. Petliura. In leading Bolshevik circles concern was regularly expressed that the Cheka was out of control; yet periodic attempts to curb it never lasted long, mainly because Lenin refused to accept that institutional checks and balances were necessary to inhibit lawlessness and corruption.

The socialist and anarchist parties proved unable to mount a concerted challenge to the burgeoning one-party dictatorship. After Kolchak's coup in November 1918, the SRs distanced themselves from the policy of overthrowing the regime by force. Most organizations agreed to make the struggle against the Whites their priority, but were unable to agree on how far they should also campaign against the Bolsheviks. At three moments of crisis in 1918–19, the Bolsheviks briefly legalized the SRs, but the tendency of policy was clear. By 1920 the majority of the Central Committee were in jail. Following the peace of Brest-Litovsk, the Left SRs also moved into opposition to the regime. In July 1918, having assassinated the German ambassador, they launched a quixotic uprising in Moscow, designed to force the Bolsheviks to break with 'opportunism'. This resulted in the party being banned, a ban that was later eased at various times. The Left SRs now succumbed to a bewildering number of splits: by October 1918 their membership had fallen by two-thirds from a peak of nearly 100,000 in June. In Ukraine the Left SRs carried out partisan activity behind Petliura's lines, but disparate groups of 'activists' – led by the redoubtable Maria Spiridonova – refused to let up on the struggle to overthrow the

Bolsheviks and to establish a 'dictatorship of toilers'. By 1920, however, the die-hards were in a minority, most of this battered party rejecting armed struggle against the regime. Splits among the Mensheviks were less damaging, but they too suffered a severe decline in membership from around 150,000 in December 1917 to under 40,000 by late 1918. A few joined the anti-Bolshevik governments in summer 1918, but the centre and left factions – the bulk of the membership – rallied in support of the Red Army, whilst seeking to defend the integrity of the soviets and trade unions. In a few soviets such as that in Tula, and in a few trade unions, such as those of printers and chemical workers, they maintained their dominance in spite of prolonged harassment by the Cheka. By autumn 1921, however, only 4,000 retained their party cards.

The Bolsheviks viewed the opposition parties with contempt, as opportunists at best, counter-revolutionaries at worst. Since they believed that only one party – their own – could represent the proletariat, other socialists and anarchists were by definition representatives of the 'petty bourgeoisie'. The decision to ban the opposition parties outright, however, was not simply an expression of ideology, since the Bolsheviks made tactical concessions to them at various junctures, even if not of a substantial or lasting kind. The Bolsheviks believed they were fighting to defend an embryonic socialist state from the forces of world imperialism. Those, like the SRs, who reserved the option of taking up arms against them, or those, like Mensheviks, who professed support for the Red Army yet reserved the right to lambast the regime, were giving succour to the enemy. As civil war intensified, Bolshevik attitudes hardened, so that what began as a pragmatic restriction hardened into a determination to be rid of the opposition parties once and for all. Yet if responsibility for the creation of one-party dictatorship lies with the Bolsheviks, that does not acquit the opposition of a measure of responsibility for its own fate. After October the opposition parties faced a scenario for which their ideologies had ill-prepared them and they fell prey to bitter and debilitating splits. They also largely failed to capitalize on the

10. Derailed train with two Red Army soldiers

widespread popular disaffection with the Bolsheviks, evident, for example, in the Left SRs' failure to oppose the deeply unpopular committees of poor peasants. This was in part, then, a failure of political leadership. Yet the opposition parties were caught by the dilemma of all civil wars, which leave little space for third parties. Despite their fury at the government, most workers and peasants identified the struggle of the Reds with defence of the revolution and when the Bolsheviks said that one was either for them or against them, it had a compelling logic.

The massive problems of recruiting, feeding, and transporting the Red Army, of squeezing grain from an unwilling peasantry, and of overcoming parochialism and inertia at the local level created irresistible pressures to centralize decision-making at the apex of the party. Moreover the constant emergencies of war fed the pressure to take instant decisions and to implement them forcefully, with the result that the party came increasingly to operate like an army. By 1919 the Central Committee of what was now known as the Russian Communist Party (bolshevik) had become the centre where all key decisions were made before being passed on to Sovnarkom or the Soviet CEC for implementation. The Central Committee was dominated by an oligarchy consisting of Lenin, Trotsky, Kamenev, Zinoviev, Stalin, and Bukharin, but there was never any doubt that Lenin was first among equals. His moral authority and his leadership skill, in particular his ability to balance intransigence with compromise, held the oligarchy together. There were no deep factional splits within the Central Committee, although a loose group did resent Trotsky's talent and influence. By 1921 the Committee had doubled in size to cope with the growing volume of business; and since its meetings were relatively infrequent, a Politburo of five, formed in 1919, dealt with the most urgent business. This met at least once a week and quickly became the most powerful decision-making body in the party-state. The sudden death from influenza in March 1919 of Ia. M. Sverdlov, the party secretary, a man of indefatigable energy, led to a rapid expansion of the Orgburo and the Secretariat. Given the party's role in directing the different agencies of government, this meant that the responsibility of the Orgburo for assigning personnel gave Stalin, its chair, extensive power.

The life-and-death struggle to preserve the state against internal counter-revolution and foreign intervention, and the relentless necessity to deal with one emergency after another led to a gradual change in the culture of the party. The paramount need to make fast decisions and get things done meant that debate and internal democracy increasingly came to be seen as luxuries. This change in culture was linked at a deeper level to the change in the nature of the party from being a conspiratorial body bent on destroying the old order, to becoming a body seeking to build and manage a state. Gradually, the range of opinion permitted in the party narrowed. By the end of the civil war, it was inconceivable that a Bolshevik should argue – as had been perfectly possible in October 1917 – that other socialist parties should be represented in the soviets or that freedom of the press should extend to 'bourgeois' publications. At the same time, as debate in a larger public sphere dried up, owing to the clampdown on the press and the elimination of opposition, so the party itself became the arena in which political conflict was played out. Factions such as the Democratic Centralists inveighed against the 'dictatorship of party officialdom' in the vain hope of reconciling centralized decision-making with rank-and-file participation in party and soviet affairs; and the Workers' Opposition rallied against attempts to reduce the trade unions to impotence. Yet the tendency for expeditious decision-making to squeeze out debate and dissent was inexorable. At the Tenth Party Congress in March 1921, against the distant roar of the Kronstadt cannons, factions were banned, supposedly as a temporary measure. The measure was never revoked.

As the party was transformed into the backbone of the new state, so it began to attract people who once would never have dreamed of becoming revolutionaries. Between the Eighth Congress in March 1919 and the Tenth, the party grew from 313,000 to 730,000, still a tiny proportion of the population. The proportion of worker members fell by about a fifth to 41%, but many of these were in fact former workers who now held positions in the state administration, economic management, or the Red Army. The rest of the membership was more or less equally divided between peasants (mostly soldiers) and white-collar employees (most of whom worked in the state apparatuses). On the eve of the Tenth Party Congress, L. B. Krasin declared:

> The source of the woes and unpleasantness we are experiencing is the fact that the Communist Party consists of 10% convinced idealists who are ready to die for the idea, and 90% hangers-on without consciences, who have joined the party in order to get a position.

Krasin was almost certainly exaggerating, but he articulated a widespread sense that the party was being hijacked by careerists. Indeed, it was precisely at this time that rank-and-file members began to attack the privileges enjoyed by 'those at the top'. What these amounted to can be seen from the diary entry for 24 November 1919 of the writer Kornei Chukovsky:

> Yesterday I was at Gorky's. Zinoviev was there. At the entrance I was amazed to see a magnificent car on the seat of which was carelessly thrown a bear skin. Zinoviev – short and fat – spoke in a hoarse and satiated voice.

Meanwhile as the state acquired ever more functions, its apparatus proliferated. By 1920 no fewer than 5.8 million people worked for the party-state. Many had worked in the same jobs before the revolution and few had much sympathy for the revolution. The army of typists, filing clerks, cashiers, accountants, storekeepers, and drivers had a low level of education, were inefficient, reluctant to take initiative, and imbued with an ethos of red tape and routinism. Officials tended to throw their weight around, whilst deferring to those above them on the bureaucratic ladder, to scramble for petty privilege, and to defend their narrow departmental turf. In the countryside, where there were fewer officials inherited from the tsarist regime, a new breed of 'soviet' official arose, many of whom had done service in the Red Army. A report from the Penza provincial Cheka in summer 1920 was typical:

> In the countryside we must quench the appetites of those 'commissars' who on going into the village consider it their sacred duty to get blind drunk, and then take other pleasures, such as raping women, shooting, and so forth.

In that year the Commissariat of State Control received tens of thousands of complaints about bribery, speculation, embezzlement, drunkenness, and sabotage mainly on the part of officials in the township soviets.

By 1920–1 there was a crisis of morale within the Communist Party. Disaffection at the trend towards authoritarianism, exemplified in the suppression of debate and the Secretariat's riding roughshod over lower-level organizations, merged with disaffection at the careerism and corruption rampant in the party-state in an anguished debate

At the beginning of September this year in the blessed town of Sergiev-Posad in Moscow province, P. V. Krutov, an old party worker and member of the militia from Bulakvoskaia township, was arrested as he was returning from a visit to the district militia headquarters in Sofrino and thrown into the guard house of the county military commissariat. This was on the whim of some 'boss' who, when asked 'Who goes there?', said 'I'm arresting you,' supposedly because he thought Krutov was a deserter who had the wrong documents. Having sat for several hours in the guard house, not knowing what was happening, comrade Krutov managed to persuade a non-party Red army soldier to bail him out so that he could personally explain to his communist comrades what had happened, and ask them to defend his honour as a Communist Party member. He went at once to the county deserters' commission where, he supposed, the documents taken from him must be. But what a genuinely 'communist defence' lay in store for him!! The chairman of the Sergiev desertion commission, the communist Kalmykov, at first tormented comrade Krutov by keeping him waiting, as happens everywhere. Then he ordered him to collect his documents from room 26, but they weren't there. When Krutov reappeared at Kalmykov's office to request his documents, Kalmykov turned into a veritable tsarist gendarme, bawling at Krutov: 'You were told to wait there. GET OUT OF HERE!' That's how 'committed communists' throw their weight about here in the provinces and consciously and precisely resurrect tsarist ways of behaviour.

Letter from S. Kriukov, Red Army soldier and party member no. 219258, to the newspaper *Bednota*, 20 September 1920 about the nature and causes of 'bureaucracy' in the new order. Both leadership and the Democratic Centralists saw it as stemming from the entry into the party-state of 'class aliens' and both agreed that the key to solving the problem lay in the promotion of workers to positions of responsibility. Neither side, however, appreciated that the major cause of 'bureaucracy' lay in the massive expansion of the party-state itself. Nor did they appreciate that proletarians promoted into official positions would not necessarily behave differently from those who had once worked for the tsarist administration, since bureaucrats derive motivation from the technical functions they perform. Where leadership and opposition parted company was over the latter's call for greater internal party democracy as a counter to bureaucracy. When the leader of the Democratic Centralists called for the Central Committee to be made more accountable, Lenin retorted:

> Soviet socialist democracy is not incompatible with one-person management or dictatorship. A dictator can sometimes express the will of a class, since he will sometimes achieve more alone and thus be more necessary.

It was a position from which he was never to retreat. Since 1917 Lenin had come to believe that centralization of power was imperative if the revolution was to be safeguarded; the most that could be allowed was for the masses to monitor those who ruled on their behalf.

Chapter 3
War Communism

After October the economy galloped from crisis to near collapse. By 1920–1 industrial output was one-fifth, average labour productivity one-third, and coal production and consumer goods production one-quarter of 1913 levels. Plummeting output, compounded by the Allied blockade and disorganization of the transport system, placed severe constraints on the Bolsheviks' room for manoeuvre. To mobilize the battered forces of industry and agriculture to meet the needs of war, they set in place policies that were retrospectively labelled 'War Communism'. These policies comprised an extremely centralized system of economic administration; the complete nationalization of industry; a state monopoly on grain and other agricultural products; a ban on private trade and the restriction of monetary-commodity exchange; rationing of key consumer items; and the imposition of military discipline on workers. Historians debate whether these policies originated in the Bolshevik intention to move as rapidly as possible towards communism, or whether they were principally dictated by the exigencies of economic collapse and civil war, rooted in expediency rather than ideology.

The Bolsheviks came to power intent on imposing state regulation on the economy, but uncertain as to how far it could be transformed along socialist lines. The Central Council of Factory Committees pressed for a Supreme Economic Council to regulate the economy and state finances, established on 2 December, together with an 'active' form of workers' control of production as an integral element of this system of economic regulation. The Decree on Workers' Control passed on 14 November – the third most popular of the Bolsheviks' founding decrees after peace and land – was obsolete within weeks as the Bolsheviks decided that the rising tide of economic chaos required that the factory committees be integrated into the more centralized apparatus of the trade unions. Initially, Lenin seems to have thought that socialist measures were on the agenda, since he ratified decrees nationalizing the banks, railways, merchant fleet, and many mines and joint-stock companies. However, during the harsh winter his enthusiasm for nationalization cooled; by March 1918 he was claiming that 'state capitalism will be our salvation', by which he meant that most enterprises would remain in private ownership but be subject to regulation by state-run cartels. This proved to be a non-starter, since few capitalists were ready to cooperate with the proletarian state. Moreover, this was precisely the time when pressure for nationalization was intensifying at the grass roots, as factory committees and soviets 'nationalized' enterprises whose owners had fled or were suspected of sabotage. Between November 1917 and March 1918, 836 enterprises were 'nationalized' from below in this way. Unable to resist this momentum, and aware that the Treaty of Brest-Litovsk made it liable to pay compensation to German nationals owning shares in private Russian companies, the government on 28 June moved decisively towards full-scale nationalization, taking some 2,000 joint-stock companies into state ownership. Henceforth the drive to nationalize proved unstoppable, fuelled mainly by the conviction that it was evidence of progress towards socialism.

After October 1917 the lamentable level of industrial productivity plunged still further as a result of wear-and-tear on machinery, supply problems and the fall in labour intensity, which was itself due to poor diet, absenteeism (brought on by the search for food and the necessity of working on the side) and, not least, by the breakdown in labour discipline. From early 1918, the trade unions struggled to combat falling productivity by restoring the piece-rate which linked wages to output.

As part of his more sober evaluation of revolutionary prospects, Lenin now pronounced that the key task facing the Russian worker was to 'learn how to work'. From spring 1918, he campaigned for a single individual to be put in charge of each enterprise, a demand that struck at the heart of workers' self-management. Throughout 1919 he faced stiff resistance from those who defended the existing system of collegial management, whereby nationalized enterprises were run by boards comprising one-third workers plus representatives of technical staff, trade unions, and state economic organs. But Lenin was never one to give up. By 1920, 82% of enterprises were under one-person management. At the same time, he campaigned for the authority of technical specialists to be restored and for them to receive salaries commensurate with their expertise, arguing that the latter was more important than 'zeal', 'human qualities', or 'saintliness'. This, too, proved deeply unpopular. As one worker told the Ninth Party Conference in September 1920: 'I'll go to my grave hating *spetsy* [technical specialists] . . . . We have to hold them in a grip of iron, the way they used to hold us.' By the end of the civil war, not much was left of the democratic forms of industrial administration promoted by the factory committees in 1917, but the government argued that this did not matter since industry had passed into the ownership of a workers' state.

During the civil war the autonomy of trade unions was also drastically curtailed. As early as January 1918 the First Trade-Union Congress rejected Menshevik demands that the unions remain 'independent', contending that in a workers' state their chief function was to 'organize production and restore the battered productive forces of the country'. From 1919, however, efforts to place workers under military discipline led to much friction between unions and government. This culminated in August 1920 in Trotsky's peremptory replacement of the elected boards of the railway and water-transport unions with a Central Committee for Transport that combined the functions of commissariat, political organ, and trade union. This sparked a fierce debate in which

Trotsky and Bukharin called for the complete absorption of the trade unions into the state; M. P. Tomsky, on behalf of the trade unions, defended a degree of trade-union autonomy but concurred that their principal task was to oversee the implementation of economic policy; and the Workers' Opposition urged that the unions be given complete responsibility for running the economy. The Tenth Party Congress in March 1921 castigated the latter view as an 'anarcho-syndicalist deviation' and gave overwhelming backing to a compromise resolution from Lenin that backed away from the idea of rapid 'statization' of the trade unions, insisting that they still had a residual function of defending workers' interests and stressing their role as 'schools of communism'.

Many of the same pressures that led to the centralization of decision-making within the party also led to hyper-centralization of the economic organs. In response to scarcity and fragmentation of power at the local level, where often a multiplicity of inexperienced soviets, economic councils, trade unions, and factory committees vied to commandeer resources and resolve local problems, the Supreme Council of the Economy struggled to impose central coordination. It was responsible chiefly for administering and financing industry, but it also intervened in the procurement and distribution of supplies, and even in transportation, food, and labour allocation. It was hardly a watchword for efficiency, being organized according to a dual principle. Boards, each with its own vertical hierarchy, presided over each branch of industry but competed with a geographically organized hierarchy of county- and province-level economic councils. In practice, this meant that dozens of overlapping and autonomous hierarchies functioned with few if any horizontal links to the relevant government commissariats. Trotsky described how in the Urals one province ate oats, while another fed wheat to horses; yet nothing could be done without the consent of the food commissariat in Moscow. On 30 November 1918 the whole system was capped by a Defence Council, vested with extraordinary powers to mobilize material and human resources for the Red Army and to coordinate the war effort at the front and in the rear. The most that can be said is that the system succeeded in targeting scarce supplies of materials, fuel, and manufactures on the Red Army. The drawbacks were that it was wasteful and hugely bureaucratic – the ratio of white-collar employees to workers in nationalized industries rising from one in ten in 1918 to one in seven in 1920.

The most critical problem facing the Bolshevik government in these years was that of food supply. To the existing reluctance of peasants to market grain were added new problems. First, the break-up of the landowners' estates strengthened subsistence farming at the expense of cash crops. Second, the loss of Ukraine deprived the Bolsheviks of a region that had produced 35% of marketed grain, and the grain area at its disposal was further cut when war came to many Volga provinces and to Siberia. Meanwhile the snarl-up on the railways, which was due to fuel shortages, the deterioration of track and rolling stock, and the devolution of control to local railway unions, meant that much of the food that was procured vanished or rotted before it reached the centres of consumption. Finally, the attempt to regulate grain supply was undermined by the boom in profiteering. The winter of 1917–18 was exceptionally severe: by early 1918 the bread ration in Petrograd was down at times to as little as 50 grams a day. In addition to the desperate efforts of workers' organizations to lay their hands on grain, profiteering by petty traders flourished. In Ivanovo-Voznesensk province so-called 'baggers' imported about 3 million puds of grain (one pud being equal to 16.5 kilograms) between 1 August 1917 and 1 January 1918, two-and-a-half times the amount procured by food authorities. Buying up grain in grain-surplus provinces for 10–12 rubles a pud, they sold it for 50–70 rubles, at a time when the fixed price was still only 3–4 rubles.

In the first months the government hoped desperately that by boosting production of goods such as fabrics, salt, sugar, and kerosene, it would

11. A country market in the 1920s

be able to induce the peasants to sell their grain. But the persisting shortage of consumer goods, together with spiralling inflation, nullified the policy. In Siberia it is reckoned that in the first half of 1918, 12 million puds of grain were requisitioned, but 25 million were converted into moonshine. Knowing that there was still plenty of grain available, on 14 May the Bolsheviks announced a 'food dictatorship' whereby all surpluses above a fixed consumption norm would be subject to confiscation. In minatory fashion the decree warned that 'enemies of the people' found to be concealing surpluses would be jailed for not less than ten years. In theory, peasants were still to be recompensed – 25% of the value of requisitions would be in the form of goods, the rest in money or credits – but according to the most generous estimate, only about half the grain requisitioned in 1919 was compensated for, and in 1920 only around 20%. Some indication of what the policy meant in practice can be gleaned from the fact that in 1918, 7,309 members of food detachments, most of them workers, were murdered as they tried to seize surpluses.

The Bolsheviks were convinced that it was 'kulaks', or wealthy peasants, who were sabotaging grain procurement, so the food dictatorship was linked to a 'war on the rural bourgeoisie'. Committees of the rural poor (kombedy) were created in the hope that poor peasants could be organized so as to provide the regime with a social base in the countryside. In reality there were relatively few peasants in the kombedy, which mainly consisted of members of the food detachments, military personnel, and party workers. This was hardly surprising given that they were closely associated with arbitrary confiscation of grain, fines, illegal arrests, and the use of force. This is not to say that there was no support at all for the kombedy. In Orel province peasants petitioned:

> Send us help, even if it is only a small Red Army detachment, so that we shall be saved from an early death from hunger . . . . We will point out to you the well-fed grain kings who shelter by their treasure chests.

We are having to work in unbelievably difficult conditions. Every peasant hides grain, digging it into the earth. Our district was one of first to deliver only because we took repressive measures against those holding it back: namely, we sat peasants in cold barns until they eventually took us to the place where the grain was hidden. But for this they arrested our comrades, the commander of the squad, and three commissars. Now we are still working but less successfully. For hiding grain we confiscate the entire herd without payment, leaving only the 12-funt hunger ration, and we send those who hide their grain to detainment in Malmysh where they have only an eighth of a funt of bread per day. The peasants call us internal enemies and look upon the food officials as beasts and as their enemies.

Report of a food-supply official, Viatka, March 1920

12. A food requisition group, 1918

But even as the kombedy were multiplying in autumn 1918, the party leadership was beginning to doubt the wisdom of the policy. In November the Sixth Congress of Soviets, commenting on the 'bitter clashes between kombedy and peasant organs of power', called for their abolition.

In January 1919 a 'turn to the middle peasantry' was accompanied by the institution of a quota assessment (*raszverstka*), whereby the food commissariat set a grain quota for each province on the basis of estimates of 'surpluses'. Formally, it introduced some predictability into requisitioning, since each county and village knew its quota; but in reality the food detachments continued to operate much as before. The amount requisitioned steadily increased, so that by the third procurement of 1920–1, 237 million puds were raised in European Russia, about 23% of gross yield. This was no more than the procurement of 1916–17, yet it represented a huge burden of suffering for the peasantry, since output had almost halved in the intervening period. In March 1920 the chair of Novgorod provincial executive committee reported: 'The province is starving. A huge number of peasants are eating moss and other rubbish.' That the specific policies of requisitioning adopted made the food crisis worse is incontrovertible, particularly given that the Bolsheviks did nothing until late in 1920 to try to halt the reduction in sown area. A less rigid policy – perhaps including elements of a tax in kind and greater reliance on the cooperative network – might have helped forestall the disaster that was building up. Nevertheless, even if the Bolsheviks had not taken a single pud of grain, peasants would still have had no incentive to market surpluses. Under Kolchak in Siberia, where there was no requisitioning, lack of manufactures and inflation caused peasants to reduce their sown areas. So it is unlikely that requisitioning could have been avoided. Fundamentally, the Bolsheviks had no choice but 'to take from the hungry to give to the hungrier', for the poor in the towns and grain-deficit provinces simply could not afford to feed themselves at free-market prices.

That said, at least half the needs of the urban population were met through the illegal and semi-legal market. Hundreds of thousands of 'baggers' scoured the countryside in search of food. The law prescribed draconian penalties for 'speculation', and 'baggers' ran the risk of arrest by the Cheka or by the road-block detachments, whose behaviour was described by the Soviet CEC as a 'shocking disgrace'. Yet the battle against private trade was never consistent, since the government knew that without it townsfolk would starve. Thus even as the nationalization of trade was being proclaimed, the authorities in the two capitals allowed peasants to sell one-and-a-half puds of food per family member on the open market. At the same time, rationing was extended in line with the long-term Bolshevik aspiration to substitute planned distribution of goods for the anarchy of the market. In July 1918 the so-called class ration was introduced in Petrograd, followed by other cities, which grouped the population into four categories. It was designed to discriminate in favour of workers and to allow the *burzhui*, in Zinoviev's words, just enough bread so that they would not forget its smell. Yet shortages meant that it was frequently impossible to fulfil the rations even of those in category one. A joke went the rounds:

13. A child's cartoon. The caption reads 'A Bolshevik is a person who doesn't want there to be any more *burzhui*.'

> A religious instruction teacher asked his secondary school: 'Our Lord fed 5,000 people with five loaves and two fishes. What is that called?' To which one wag replied: 'The ration system'.

Inability to meet rations fuelled pressure on groups to get themselves into a higher category. By April 1920 in Petrograd, 63% of the population was in category one and only 0.1% in the lowest category. Rationing also fed corruption: by 1920 there were 10 million more ration cards in circulation than members of the urban population.

A terrifying crisis was building up, yet the scent of victory caused the Bolsheviks by 1920 to believe that the draconian methods used to win the civil war could be turned to the construction of socialism. Trotsky was the most enthusiastic exponent of the idea that 'obligation and compulsion' could be used to 'reconstruct economic life on the basis of a single plan'. Not all Bolsheviks were enamoured of the idea of the labour army as a microcosm of socialist society, but for the best part of a year, the leadership committed itself to a vision of army and economy fused into a single, all-embracing military-economic body. During the first half of 1920 as many as 6 million people were drafted to work in cutting timber and peat. In March – with absenteeism on the railways running between 20% and 40% – Trotsky took over the Commissariat of Transport and set about imposing militarization on the workforce. This was a fortress built on shifting sand, however, since in some sectors 'labour desertion' ran as high as 90%. In a similar way, some now hailed the fact that black market prices were running at thousands of times their 1917 level as a sign that money was about to disappear, a sign of the arrival of communism. Lenin cautioned that 'it is impossible to abolish money at once', yet the effort to stabilize the currency and maintain money taxes now gave way to a plan to replace currency with 'labour units' and 'energy units'. In the first half of 1920, 11 million people, including 7.6 million children, ate for free in public canteens, where food was meagre and badly cooked and conditions often filthy. Later in the year, payments for housing, heating, lighting, public transport, the postal service, medical care, theatre, and cinema were abolished, although this was motivated as much by practical concern at the relative cost of collecting payment for these services as by a desire to abolish money *per se*. Indeed the process of 'naturalizing' the economy took place almost entirely independently of the will of the Bolsheviks; what was distinctive was that they now seized on this as evidence that the transition to socialism was well underway.

Over the winter of 1920–1 such euphoria was rapidly dispelled. The Volga region, which in 1919–20 had supplied almost 60% of grain procurements, was hit by drought in summer 1920. The drought grew worse in 1921 and by summer it was estimated that 35 million people in an area centred on the Volga, but including parts of southern Ukraine,

Kazakhstan, and western Siberia, were in the grip of famine. Its severity was compounded by the cut-back in agricultural production, by losses of livestock and equipment due to war, by breakdown in transport and, of course, by requisitioning. As many as 6 million may have died, not only from starvation but from scurvy, dysentery, and typhus. The Commissariat of Enlightenment received grotesque reports that mothers were tying their children to separate corners of their huts for fear that they would eat each other.

In October 1921 Lenin finally conceded that War Communism had been a mistake, claiming that it had been dictated by 'desperate necessity' and also, rather confusingly, 'an attempt to introduce the socialist principles of production and distribution by "direct assault"'. There can be little doubt that the collapse of industry, chaos in the transport system, and the destruction wrought by war placed severe constraints on the Bolsheviks' room for manoeuvre. Moreover, the war determined that grain procurement and industrial production be concentrated on the needs of the Red Army rather than consumers. That circumstances of war did much to dictate policy can be seen from the fact that even White regimes, committed to the free market, resorted to measures of economic compulsion in the 'interests of state'. Moreover, policies, whether carefully crafted or hastily cobbled together, threw up entirely unintended consequences that set parameters for future action. The imposition of fixed prices on agricultural products, for example, a policy introduced by the tsarist regime, did much to stoke hyperinflation which, in turn, served to undermine the ruble. Nevertheless if structural constraints and contingencies did much to shape the policies that constituted War Communism, one may not conclude that those policies were simply the outcome of 'desperate necessity'. Policy choices were not unilaterally 'imposed' by objective circumstances: they were defined by the dominant conceptions and inherited dispositions of the Bolshevik party, sometimes as matters of explicit choice, sometimes as unconscious reflexes. Antipathy towards the market, and the equation of state

14. Famine 1921–2

ownership and state regulation with communism all served to determine the policy choices taken. Lenin may have concluded that War Communism was an error, but the command-administrative system and militarized ideology that it engendered proved to be lasting elements of the Soviet system.

Looting the looters

The collapse of industry and the grave food shortages led to the breakdown of urban life. Between 1917 and 1920, the percentage of the population living in towns fell from 18% to 15%, but the population of Petrograd fell by almost 70% and that of Moscow by half. The desperate search for food forced people to truck and barter and to pillage furniture, wooden fences, any available tree to stay warm. The literary critic V. Shklovsky wrote: 'People who lived in housing with central heating died in droves. They froze to death – whole apartments of them.' It was against this background of extraordinary crisis that the centuries-old division between propertied Russia and the toiling masses was wiped out in a matter of months. Seldom has history seen so precipitate and so total a destruction of a ruling class. In its editorial to mark New Year 1919, *Pravda* proclaimed:

> Where are the wealthy, the fashionable ladies, the expensive restaurants and private mansions, the beautiful entrances, the lying newspapers, all the corrupted 'golden life'? All swept away.

The nationalization of industry and the banks constituted the principal mechanism through which the assets of the capitalists were expropriated. In the countryside, of course, the peasants turfed the landowners off their estates although not infrequently they allowed them to stay in their ancestral homes. In addition, soviets and Chekas, strapped for cash and obsessed with putting 'all power into the hands of the localities', exacted 'contributions' and 'confiscations' from those they considered *burzhui*. In Tver' the soviet demanded sums ranging from 20,000 to 100,000 rubles from local traders and industrialists, threatening to send them to Kronstadt if they did not comply. Given the weakness of the local authorities, such expropriations were often barely distinguishable from banditry, as the leading Chekist M. I. Latsis conceded:

> Our Russian figures: 'Don't I really deserve those pants and boots that the bourgeoisie have been wearing until now! That's a reward for my work, right? So, I'll take what's mine.'

Hit by 'requisitions', forced to share their apartments with poor families and to do humiliating work assignments, landowners, capitalists, and tsarist officials sold what they could, packed their belongings, and headed for White areas or abroad. Between 1917 and 1921, 1.8 million to 2 million emigrated, overwhelmingly from the educated and propertied groups. A surprising number, however, chose to hang on: A. A. Golovin, scion of an ancient family, worked in the garage of the Malyi Theatre in 1921 and his son went on to become famous for his film portrayals of Stalin. These 'former people' – a term once applied to criminals – struggled to conceal their origins and to steer clear of politics. Yet despite their severe reduction in circumstance, they continued to be viewed with mistrust by the regime, seen as the potential fifth column for a White-Guard restoration.

For the multifarious middle classes, opportunities to adapt to the new order were more plentiful, although the revolution also brought a sharp diminution in their privileges. While Lenin despised the intelligentsia, he was quick to understand that the revolution could not survive without 'knowledgeable, experienced, businesslike people'. As well as paying engineers relatively high salaries, doctors, dentists, architects, and other professionals were allowed to practise privately. Nor was it unusual for former factory owners to sit on the industrial-branch boards of the Supreme Economic Council or for former merchants to work for the supply organs. Those with some education found jobs in the soviet and party apparatus – as clerks, secretaries, minor functionaries – which entitled them to the second-grade food ration ('responsible' soviet officials qualified for the first). For the far more numerous lower-middle strata who lacked saleable skills the principal means of survival was through petty trade and artisanal production.

The intelligentsia was the only elite group to survive the revolution intact, though its self-image was badly shaken. Most were moderate socialists in sympathy, but the war and revolution had killed any naïve belief in the innate goodness of the people. Their sense of themselves as the conscience of society, called upon to oppose tyranny, led most to oppose the Bolshevik seizure of power. They deplored the strident demagogy of the new rulers, the violence, the closure of the press, the lawlessness on the streets. Most had had enough of politics and took a neutral stance in the civil war. Most were not well paid and few had reserves to fall back on. The composer A. T. Grechaninov recalled: 'my health was undermined to such an extent that I could hardly drag my feet. My hands suffered from frost bite and I could not touch the piano.' Morale, however, was not necessarily as low as one might assume. N. Berdiaev, elected to a professorship of philosophy at Moscow University in 1920 – where 'I gave lectures in which I openly and without hindrance criticized Marxism' – did not mind labour conscription:

> I did not feel at all depressed and unhappy despite the unaccustomed strain of the pick and shovel on my sedentary muscles . . . I could not help realizing the justice of my predicament.

The Bolsheviks came to power bent on disestablishing and dispossessing the Orthodox Church, which had been a key pillar of the old order. Church and state were separated, church lands were nationalized, state subsidies were withdrawn, religious education was outlawed in schools, and religion was made a 'private matter'. The response of the new patriarch of the Church, Tikhon, was crushing: in

January 1918 he pronounced an anathema on the Bolsheviks, warning that they would 'burn in hell in the life hereafter and be cursed for generations'. The ending of financial subventions hit the central and diocesan administrations hard, but made little difference to parish clergy, who were generally provided with an allotment of land and some financial support by parishioners. By late 1920, 673 monasteries – 'powerful screws in the exploiting machine of the old ruling classes' – had been liquidated and their land confiscated. Violent clashes between supporters of the Church and of soviet power were a constant of the civil war. Bolshevik propaganda portrayed priests as drunkards and gluttons, and monks and nuns as sinister 'black crows'. For their part, most of hierarchy portrayed the Bolsheviks as Christ-haters, German hirelings, 'Jewish-Masonic slave-masters'. Tikhon urged the faithful to resist the Bolsheviks only by spiritual means, but many clergy sided openly with the Whites. Bolshevik supporters, particularly sailors and soldiers, meted out horrible repression: in 1918–19, 28 bishops and several hundred clergy were killed.

The class structure of tsarist Russia buckled under the blows of war, economic collapse, and revolutionary attack. Yet having overturned Russia's somewhat fragile class structure, the Bolsheviks chose to use the discourse of class to define and organize the new social world, backing it up with the panoply of material and symbolic resources at the disposal of the state. They projected the civil war as a life-and-death struggle between international capital and the workers and toiling peasants of the world. The speeches of activists were studded with images of revolutionary conflagrations, of counter-revolutionary hydras and capitalist jackals. Though much propaganda was couched in language that ordinary folk could barely understand, the discourse played upon demotic understandings of class that had been so visible in 1917, mobilizing deep-seated animosity between 'us' and 'them'.

Popular rebellion

Peasant unrest was a persistent thorn in the side of the regime. Most uprisings were small-scale, sparked by food requisitioning, conscription, the abuses of soviet officials or kombedy, or by labour obligations. In 1919 most of the hundreds of uprisings were spontaneous, uniting peasants of all strata, with little in the way of a political goal. By far the largest was the 'kaftan' (*chapanny*) rebellion, which welled up in Samara and Simbirsk after the imposition of an emergency revolutionary tax in March. At its peak it involved over 100,000, some of whom established links with Kolchak. The largest of the uprisings of 1920, the 'pitchfork' (*vilochnoe*) uprising, was centred on the Tatars of Ufa but spread into the Volga region, where requisitioning was concentrated. In Samara the 'black eagle uprising', which formed a part of the 'pitchfork' insurgency, revealed a degree of politicization: 'We are the peasant millions. Our enemies are the communists. They drink our blood and oppress us like slaves.' Peasant insurgents frequently behaved in bestial fashion. In Penza in March 1920 the local commissar had his nose cut off, then his ears, then his head. A report concluded: 'Now everything is peaceful and quiet. The peasants were calmed with the help of the lash.' As this suggests, the Bolsheviks retaliated ruthlessly against what they saw as the work of 'kulaks', 'counter-revolutionaries', and 'Black Hundreds'. The kaftan rebels killed about 200 officials, but the punitive detachments sent to quell them killed 1,000 rebels in combat and executed a further 600. Some historians lump all forms of peasant resistance into a single 'Green movement'; but this elides important distinctions. When the Soviet authorities talked of 'Greens' they referred to the roving bands of deserters who lived in the fields and forests, surviving through banditry and attacks on requisition squads. These bands were more structured and politicized than most peasant rebels. Generally, they could rely on the sympathy of villagers, but whenever they tried to organize the latter into more permanent formations or to involve them into compulsory labour duties, they risked provoking their animosity.

With the elimination of the White threat, peasant protest escalated to dramatically new levels. In 1921 there were over 50 large-scale peasant uprisings in regions as far-flung as Ukraine and Belorussia, the north Caucasus and Karelia. In Tambov A. S. Antonov, a former Left SR who had served the soviet cause with distinction until summer 1918, built an army of 40,000 partisans that controlled practically the entire territory of the Volga by February 1921. The army had territorial divisions and hierarchies of command, supply lines based on the villages, and 'unions of toiling peasantry' as its political back-up. The latter demanded the overthrow of 'Communist-Bolshevik power, which has brought the country to poverty, destruction, and disgrace'; political equality for all citizens; the calling of a Constituent Assembly; socialization of land; and partial denationalization of factories under workers' control. In western Siberia partisans overthrew Bolshevik power across 1 million square kilometres and severed railway contact with European Russia. On 21 February 1921 they seized the city of Tobolsk and formed a soviet which proclaimed civil liberties, free trade, equal rations, denationalization of industry, and the restoration of the old courts. There were at least 100,000 fighting men, but the different divisions were never subject to a unified command. Not until autumn did the Red Army regain control. In a loose way the different peasant movements saw themselves united in a common cause. The Antonov partisans, for example, fought in expectation that the supporters of Makhno would come to their aid from Ukraine, even though Makhno had by this stage fled to Romania. The political influence of the SRs was everywhere in evidence; but although there were a fair number of demands for the return of the Constituent Assembly, the most widespread slogan was for 'soviets without communists'. Convinced that the 'toiler-and-peasant government has long since ceased to exist', rebels wished to see the communist regime overthrown; yet they remained powerfully drawn to the soviet idea, which they associated with the overthrow of the landlords and rule by the toilers.

Between 1917 and 1920 the number of factory and mine workers fell

In the purely peasant and semi-proletarian provinces soviet power in general and the Communist Party in particular has no social base. You will not find there broad layers of the population who are committed to us, who share our programme, and are ready to act for us. I am not speaking about kulaks or the remnants of the bourgeoisie, of which hardly any remain. I am talking about the broad mass of workers, artisans, and, especially, peasants. We have contrived to frighten off the mass of middle and poor peasants. Voluntary mobilization has failed. We met with the refusal of entire trade unions to give up even one man. And matters with the peasantry were entirely antipathetic. I do not say that these are consciously counter-revolutionary forces, they are not. But the mass of the population is indifferent or hostile to our party. In many districts they are waiting for Kolchak. It's true that when he arrives the mood changes to our benefit, but not for long. The reasons for this are many. But the central fact – and this is true on a national level – is that we have actually given nothing to the peasants except hardship. Terror reigns. We hold on only through terror.

Report of Iu. M. Steklov, editor of *Pravda*, to the Central Committee, June 1919

from 3.6 million to 1.5 million. Over a million workers returned to their villages, several hundred thousand departed for the Red Army, and tens of thousands left to take up administrative and managerial positions in the soviet, trade-union, and party organs. Workers suffered a huge drop in living standards. By 1920 the real value of the average 'wage' was reckoned to be 38% of the 1913 level, although this was made up largely of rations, free housing, transport, clothing, and other goods. At the same time, elements of coercion and hierarchy were being reintroduced into the workplace. Not surprisingly, therefore, worker discontent was rife. The Bolsheviks explained this as being the result of 'declassing', i.e.

the strengthening of 'petty-bourgeois elements' in the working class. It is true that many of their most ardent supporters left the factories; but within a much depleted workforce the ratio between the core of skilled and experienced workers and the larger group of less skilled, less experienced women and recent recruits probably remained about the same as it had been in 1917.

As early as spring 1918, worker support for the government started rapidly to ebb, as unemployment, food shortages, and declining wages began to bite. Mounting bitterness manifested itself in a revival of support for Mensheviks and SRs. From early March in Tula, Petrograd, and elsewhere Mensheviks formed assemblies of factory plenipotentiaries to campaign for civil rights, independent trade unions, and free soviet elections, with the ultimate aim of reconvening the Constituent Assembly. In Petrograd, where the movement was strongest, the Assembly had 200 delegates, who claimed to represent two-thirds of the city's workforce. The Cheka foiled a plan by 'this group of pretenders and counter-revolutionaries' to call a general strike on 2 July; but it is clear that their support was by no means firm. As the plenipotentiaries conceded, worker grievances were predominantly about unemployment, bread rations, and freedom to leave the city in order to search for food: 'the masses have still not turned away from the Bolsheviks and are not completely disenchanted.'

The 'democratic counter-revolution' received the support of many workers. N. I. Podvoisky, chair of the Supreme Military Inspectorate, reported from the Volga provinces:

> With rare exceptions workers are hostile to soviet power. Unemployed from the demobilized factories are the most hostile towards us and a certain number of workers at the Pipe and Cartridge factories in Samara have gone over to the Cossacks.

At Izhevsk in Viatka province SR Maximalists in the Red Guard so alienated the local populace with their requisitions, searches, and arrests that the Mensheviks and SRs triumphed in the soviet elections in May 1918, prompting the Bolsheviks to shut the soviet down. When the Czech Legion approached on 5 August the SR-dominated veterans' association, backed by workers from the huge munitions plant, seized control of the town. Thousands of workers, including those at the neighbouring Votkinsk works, joined the People's Army, which was defeated by the Reds in mid-November, some later joining Kolchak. The most violent confrontation between Bolsheviks and workers, however, occurred in Astrakhan, a fishing town on the lower Volga in a strategically very sensitive area. On 10 March 1919 striking metallurgical workers, demanding free trade and an increase in food rations, clashed with sailors. A crowd, including deserters from the 45th regiment, then attacked the Communist headquarters, killing several officials. S. Kirov, chair of the military revolutionary committee, ordered 'the merciless extermination of the White Guard swine' and in several days' fighting a couple of thousand insurgents were slaughtered. Yet in general workers loathed the Whites, who were energetic in suppressing trade unions and restoring factory owners to power in the areas under their control. Following Kolchak's coup in November 1918, there was a spate of political strikes and disturbances in the cities and mining regions of Siberia. The strike by miners in Cheremkhovo in December 1919 signalled a turning-point in Red fortunes. In the Donbas, too, where General S. V. Denisov had hundreds of miners in Iuzivka hanged, the Whites were equally detested.

The crystallization of the civil war into a struggle between Reds and Whites had the effect of firming up worker support for the Red cause, but that is not to say that it was ever solid. Throughout the civil war there were regular stoppages, mostly limited in scope and duration. In 1920 in 18 provinces under Red control there were 146 strikes involving 135,000 workers, most of them provoked by problems of food supply. By spring 1920, over 1 million were on special rations, yet on average these were fulfilled by only a quarter or a fifth. Such stoppages cannot be dismissed simply as 'economic', since workers now depended on the state for the fulfilment of their basic needs. The strikes, therefore, inevitably had political implications, which frequently took the form of attacks on the privileges of officials: 'the communists receive high salaries and food rations, eat three dishes in their canteens, while we are given slops as though we were pigs'. Furthermore, the fanatical way in which the regime dealt with strikes further politicized them. In 1920, after the civil war was over, the chair of the provincial party committee in Ekaterinoslav reported:

> 'In September the workers here rose up against the despatch to the countryside of food detachments. We decided to pursue an iron policy. We closed down the tram park, fired all workers and employees, and sent some of them to the concentration camp; those of the appropriate age we sent to the front, others we handed over to the Cheka.'

This may have been an extreme response, but confiscation of strikers' ration cards, deployment of armed force, and mass dismissals followed by selective rehiring were standard weapons in the Bolshevik arsenal.

The Bolsheviks saw the hand of the opposition behind any outbreak of worker unrest and their response was invariably to arrest workers known to be SRs or Mensheviks. While it is doubtful that the latter were in a position to instigate worker protest, they were able to exert political influence. On 10 March 1919 Putilov workers, angry at the absence of bread, passed a Left SR resolution by 10,000 votes to 22, excoriating the 'servile yoking of workers to the factories' and calling for the destruction of the 'commissarocracy'. Yet support for the opposition was basically an expression of anger and frustration rather than of principled commitment. Attitudes were volatile and the same workers could react in different ways at different times. So long as civil war dragged on, it is fair to say that in spite of their deep disaffection, workers showed no desire to jeopardize the operations of the Red Army.

Thus when Iudenich, the White general, threatened Petrograd in autumn 1920, many worked a 16-hour day to defeat him. Moreover, if it only took a handful of oppositionists to give political form to economic discontent, it often simply required the party to send in agitators and extra supplies to dispel support for the opposition. At the beginning of 1920, the Menshevik leader L. Martov conceded:

> So long as we branded Bolshevism, we were applauded; as soon as we went on to say that a changed regime was needed to fight Denikin successfully our audience turned cold or even hostile.

Doubtless a minority believed that the regime had comprehensively betrayed the revolution; but the attitudes of the majority were more contradictory. Many ideals of the revolution had bitten deep: workers evinced fierce hostility to *burzhui*, a strong belief in equality, hatred of privilege – not least when enjoyed by communists – and broad support for the soviet idea. When judged against these ideals, the Bolsheviks were found wanting; yet most workers were not convinced that the opposition provided a credible alternative.

The sailors and soldiers of Kronstadt, an island in the Gulf of Finland, some 30 kilometres from Petrograd, put their lives on the line for the ideals of 1917. On 1 March 1921, 16,000 of them passed a resolution calling for the dismantling of War Communism, the devolution of power to freely elected soviets, for freedoms of speech, the press, and association. There was no express call for the overthrow of soviet power, although once the rebels were under siege some did adopt that aim. Perhaps 12,000 out of 18,000 military and 8,000 to 9,000 adult male civilians out of a total civilian population of 30,000 threw in their lot with the rebels. The Bolsheviks responded decisively. On 7 March military operations to suppress the rebellion began, but effective leadership from professional officers on the island meant that the Reds were repulsed with heavy losses. Only on 17 March were 45,000 Red troops ready to launch an assault; by the following day the island was in

Bolshevik hands. Since 700 Soviet troops had been killed and 2,500 injured, reprisals against the rebels were harsh. By summer 1921, 2,103 prisoners had been sentenced to death – though the actual number shot was in the hundreds – and 6,459 sentenced to imprisonment. The Bolsheviks portrayed the rebellion as a 'White Guard plot'. Certainly, White agents sought to exploit the rebellion; but the rebels' dream of local autonomy and their loathing of privilege were anathema to the Whites. Moreover, they turned down a request by Chernov, the SR leader, to visit the island. The Bolsheviks were probably right to think that had the rebels succeeded, it would have led either to the disintegration of the state or to a White restoration. The real choice was still between a Red or a White dictatorship. That said, the Bolsheviks could have dealt with the rebels in a less bloody fashion. It was not clear that they wanted armed confrontation and there was a reasonable chance for compromise, given that the Bolsheviks could have offered an end to War Communism as a quid pro quo. Yet they would brook no compromise. Curiously, their intransigence seems to have arisen less from confidence, even though the rising was poorly timed and ill-prepared, than from insecurity. Knowing how deeply hated they were, the Bolsheviks sensed that any show of weakness would encourage rebels elsewhere. By suppressing the sailors of Kronstadt they bade farewell to the most cherished – and utopian – ideals of 1917. Henceforward nothing further would be heard of power to the soviets, workers' self-management, or a democratic army: the nature of the revolution had changed for good.

The political developments of the civil war defied every Bolshevik expectation. In October 1917 when the worker A. V. Shotman ventured to doubt whether 'even a cook or housekeeper' could administer the state, as Lenin had claimed in *State and Revolution*, he rounded on him: 'Rubbish! Any worker will master any ministry within a few days.' Yet in 1920 an exasperated Lenin exclaimed: 'Does every worker really know how to run the state? Practical people know that this is a fairy story.' As the Bolsheviks metamorphosed from a party of insurrection into a party of government, their perspective on reality changed. As early as August 1918, in a deliberate pitch to those ready to support any government so long as it could guarantee they would not be shot or robbed on the street, Bukharin wrote an article in *Pravda* entitled 'Order' (*Poriadok*). By 1921 the Bolsheviks had built a rudimentary state, but one that was the antithesis of the commune state of which Lenin had once dreamed. By 1920 the basic features of the Communist system were in place: rule by a single party, extreme centralization of power, intolerance of dissent, the curtailment of independent organizations, and readiness to use force to solve political and economic tasks. The efficiency of the state at this stage should not be exaggerated. In practice, it was a ramshackle set of competing party and state structures, permeated by arbitrariness, commandism, and inefficiency, that depended for its functioning not only on peremptory decrees from the centre but on powerful bosses and their cliques at the local level. Nevertheless, against the odds, a revolutionary vanguard, cut off from its mass base, had built a state, using the party apparatus, the army, coercion, and propaganda.

Historians debate the extent to which the party-state came into being as the result of Bolshevik ideology or the pressures of civil war. Some argue that the seeds of Bolshevik tyranny lay in the Marxist notion of the dictatorship of the proletariat; others in Lenin's notion of the vanguard party with its implication that the party knew what was best for the working class. Such fundamental tenets certainly played a part in bringing an authoritarian party-state into being. Yet the civil war was as much about certain principles being jettisoned as about others being confirmed. The decentralized vision of socialism associated with 1917 – soviet democracy, workers' self-management – was permanently sidelined. State, party, and army – not the soviets or factory committees – now came to be seen as the bearers of revolution. The fact that ideology evolved in this way suggests that it was not the sole or even paramount driving force behind the creation of the party dictatorship. If the seeds of dictatorship lay in ideology, they only came to fruition in the face of the remorseless demands placed on party and state by civil war and economic collapse.

The culture of the party was profoundly changed by civil war. The atmosphere of pervasive violence and destruction, the unremitting popular hostility, sharpened dictatorial and brutal reflexes. The Bolshevik ethos had always been one of ruthlessness, authoritarianism, and 'class hatred', but in the context of civil war these qualities transmogrified into cruelty, fanaticism, and absolute intolerance of those who thought differently. The invasion of foreign powers, the failure of revolution to spread across Europe, bred a mentality of encirclement, of Russia as an armed fortress, as well as an obsession with enemies: 'The enemy keeps watch over us and is ready at any minute to exploit our every blunder, mistake, or gesture of vacillation.' The fact that the Bolsheviks achieved victory in the war – albeit at a punishing cost – strengthened illusions of infallibility. It was such attitudes that increasingly came to define the party. The change in culture, though not a direct expression of ideology, was easily justified in terms of it. As M. S. Ol'minsky told the Ninth Party Conference in 1920: Old Bolsheviks understood that the sacrifice of democracy was dictated by the emergency of war; 'but many of our comrades understand the destruction of all democracy as the last word in communism, as real communism'.

Finally, the civil war saw the hardening conviction that the state was the modality through which socialism would be built. Lenin's ideology – his absolutization of the state as an instrument of class rule – was at the root of this process. But the hypertrophy of the party-state was as much the result of improvisation in the face of crises and unforeseen developments as of wilful intention. Indeed ideology in many respects left the Bolsheviks powerless to make sense of the forces that were shaping their regime, nowhere more so than in their primitive understanding of 'bureaucracy'. Having eliminated private ownership of the means of production with astounding ease, Lenin became convinced that the state alone was the guarantor of progress to socialism. Proletarian power was guaranteed exclusively by the state and had nothing to do, for example, with the nature of authority relations in the workplace. Lenin thus had no inkling that the state itself could become an instrument of exploitation and little insight into how the Bolsheviks themselves could be 'captured' by the apparatus they notionally controlled.

Chapter 4
NEP: politics and
the economy

In March 1921 Lenin told the Tenth Party Congress that Russia was like a man 'beaten to within an inch of his life'. The Congress, in session as the Kronstadt rebellion was underway, took place against a background of utter devastation in the economy and nation-wide peasant insurgency. Many feared that the regime might not survive. The response of Congress was to endorse a policy that had been urged by some in the party for well over a year: the abandonment of forced requisitioning in favour of a tax in kind on the peasantry, calculated as a percentage of the harvest. This relatively modest step marked the inauguration of the New Economic Policy (NEP), which soon turned into a wholescale repudiation of War Communism. Following the Congress, the Soviet CEC made clear that grain surpluses might be sold to cooperatives or on the open market (the word 'trade' was still taboo). Rationing and state distribution of subsistence items were soon dismantled; and cooperatives and private individuals were permitted to lease small-scale enterprises. Later, in response to the so-called 'scissors crisis' – which saw the 'blades' of industrial and agricultural prices open ever wider to the point where in October 1923 the ratio of the former to the latter stood at three times the 1913 level – the government imposed stringent fiscal, credit, and price measures to cut industrial prices. This entailed slashing public expenditure and subsidies to state enterprises. By 1924 a stable currency had been established in which the ruble was backed by gold. Full NEP was now in place: a hybrid, evolving system that combined a peasant economy, a state sector subject to 'commercial accounting', private trade and industry, a state and cooperative network of procurement and distribution, a credit system, and a rudimentary capital market.

In the jargon of the day, the aim of NEP was to cement the alliance between the proletariat and the peasantry. Lenin spoke of it both as a 'retreat' and as a policy intended to last 'seriously and for a long time'. In his last writings, penned when he was already seriously ill, he seemed to sketch a scenario in which the transition to socialism would be a gradual one, based upon cultural revolution (see Chapter 5) and the expansion of cooperatives among the peasantry, even going so far as to concede that 'there has been a radical modification in our whole outlook on socialism'. Historians argue over the significance of these valedictory meditations. Some see them as evidence that Lenin had come to embrace a semi-liberal, market-based alternative to statist socialism, in which the Soviet Union would evolve gradually from state capitalism to socialism. Others point out that neither he nor his party ever deviated from a conception of socialism as the elimination of the market and complete state ownership of the means of production. What is clear is that Lenin came to see NEP as more than a 'retreat', as a transitional system in which market mechanisms would gradually strengthen the state sector at the expense of the private sector over at least 'one or two decades'. All leading Bolsheviks came to accept that NEP was more than a temporary retreat, but they disagreed violently about the nature and duration of this transition period.

The economic year 1925–6 marked the apogee of NEP, this being the time when official policy, as articulated by Bukharin and backed by Stalin, was at its most favourable to the peasantry, particularly to the kulaks. The leadership announced that taxes were to be lowered and subsequently restrictions on hiring labour and leasing land were relaxed. In 1923–4 the tax in kind had been commuted into an exclusively money tax levied on cultivated land, cattle, and horses. It operated on a progressive basis: in 1924–5 one-fifth of households were exempt on the grounds that they were poor peasants and by 1929 this proportion had risen to one-third. Overall, the level of direct taxation on farm incomes increased in comparison with the pre-war period; but since land rents had been abolished, the combined burden of indirect and direct taxes fell from 19% in 1913 to just under 10% in 1926–7. By that year, grain production had recovered to its pre-war level and output of non-grain products was well above pre-war levels. Yet all was not as well as it seemed. The fundamental purpose of NEP – notwithstanding all the mollifying talk about the peasantry – was to squeeze the rural sector in order to raise the capital necessary for industrial investment. In particular, the government wished to export grain – which in fact accounted for only 35% of net agricultural produce in 1926 – in order to pay for imports of machinery. To its alarm, however, the peasants were still marketing less grain than before the war, preferring to use it to feed the growing rural population and rebuild livestock herds. The government responded by raising procurement targets and moving from procurement through the market to procurement by state and cooperative organs. After January 1928, it behaved as though grain were state property.

During the period of NEP, the underlying resilience and traditionalism of agriculture made itself powerfully felt. The land revolution had reversed the long-term decline in communal land use, the commune even spreading to new areas such as Ukraine. Agriculture remained woefully primitive, with equipment such as horse-drawn sowing machines, harvesters, mowers, and threshing machines extremely rare. The robustness of the commune was a factor inhibiting mechanization and government efforts to encourage genuine collective farms. Yet it would be an error to conclude that peasant society had sunk back into time-honoured ways. By 1928 nearly half of peasant households were members of consumer cooperatives, and agronomists and land surveyors continued the process, begun by Stolypin, of reorganizing land in a more rational and equitable fashion, mainly to the benefit of the neediest households. Peasant attitudes to farming were not monolithic: traditional orientations prevailed, yet the burning question of land had ceased to absorb the younger generation in the way it had their parents. A sample of letters from the 1.3 million sent to the *Peasant Newspaper* between 1924–6 presents a complex picture. Nearly 60% of letters reflect a preference for collective over individual forms of enterprise but see the gradual development of cooperatives as most in tune with Russian ways; and while not antagonistic to the market, they urge the state to help agriculture through taxation and subsidies. The rest of the letters divide more or less equally into three categories: those that are mistrustful of the state and advocate individual entrepreneurship as the only way to improve peasant living standards; those – overwhelmingly from poor peasants – that bemoan continuing inequalities and look to the state to rectify these; and those – whose authors include communists and members of agrarian communes – that are genuinely enthusiastic for collective farms. All this suggests that change was taking place in agriculture. The problem was that it was too slow to sustain the rapid modernization that the regime wished to see.

Industry and labour

The struggle with more advanced capitalist states that had been a key element in the civil war, combined with an apocalyptic sense that socialist Russia was destined to outstrip the capitalist West, helped during the early 1920s to redefine the nature of the revolution as one against socio-economic and cultural backwardness. NEP saw the Bolsheviks discard the illusion that revolution in the advanced capitalist world would come to their aid and forced them to accept that they would have to pull themselves up by their own boot-straps. The paramount goals were to industrialize, urbanize, modernize agriculture, and bring education and prosperity to the Soviet people. These objectives were not fundamentally different from those of the late tsarist regime, and the end of the 1920s was to see a revival of the traditional Russian pattern of state-induced transformation of society, driven by military and economic competition with the West. Yet the ideology that articulated these goals was historically new. In contrast to capitalist industrialization, socialist industrialization was to be carried out on a rational basis, by means of specialization, universal norms, and a 'single economic plan', about which there had been much talk since 1917. A new strain in Bolshevik ideology, which may be termed 'productivist', now came to the fore. This put the development of the productive forces and the planned organization of production at the heart of the socialist vision. It emphasized the role of science and technology in building socialism. Productivism was evident in Lenin's enthusiasm for electrification, which he avowed would 'produce a decisive victory of the principles of communism in our country' by transforming small-scale agriculture, by eliminating drudgery from the home, and by dramatically improving public health and sanitation.

NEP stimulated a rapid recovery of industry: by 1926–7, production in large-scale industry surpassed the pre-war level and the total number employed in industry (3.1 million), construction (0.2 million), and railways (0.9 million) was roughly the same as in 1913. However, NEP proved far more successful in stimulating light industry than the heavy industry that Russia so badly needed if it were to become a strong industrial power. Moreover, once existing factories had been restored to normal working, it was not clear that NEP could generate the level of capital necessary for the rapid construction of new factories, mines, and oil installations. In spite of privatization of small industry, nearly all large industry, together with the banks and wholesale trade, remained in state ownership. Indeed most workers – as many as four-fifths of Moscow's workforce – continued to be employed in the state enterprises. The latter were supposed to be self-financing, allowed to buy, sell, and enter into contracts, but in practice, they relied upon state subsidies. The Supreme Economic Council and the finance commissariat, together with the new State Planning Commission, influenced industrial investment by fixing wholesale prices, allocating credit, regulating wages, and controlling imports, and by means of the annual state plan ('control figures'). The result was that industrial costs and prices remained high: in 1926 they were roughly twice as high as in 1913, although subsequently there was some reduction. Net investment in industry did rise – to a level about one-fifth higher than in 1913 – but at the expense of investment in housing and transport. Moreover, it has been reckoned that two-thirds of growth was financed out of the state budget, quite inadequate for a poor country facing competition from much stronger neighbours. The record of NEP was thus contradictory. By 1928 gross national income had recovered to its pre-war level, but the gap in production per head between the Soviet Union and the advanced capitalist countries was as wide as ever.

With NEP the tight controls over labour associated with militarization were lifted, but managerial hierarchies were fully restored. The overriding task of the 'Red Directors' – nearly two-thirds of whom were technical and managerial specialists – was to revive production; and the secretaries of the party cell and the factory trade-union committee were expected to cooperate fully to achieve this. The unions lost their voice in policy-making, but could still contest management decisions through the rates-and-disputes commissions and the courts. The power of the foreman on the shop floor was substantially restored, and instances of foremen behaving rudely to workers, demanding bribes and sexual favours soon resurfaced. In spite of the emphasis on technical and managerial know-how, *spetsy* (technical specialists) remained suspect in the eyes of both workers and the regime. In 1927 miners in Shakhty in the Donbas rebelled against new production targets under the rallying-cry, 'Beat the Communists and the Specialists.' The following year the regime cynically exploited such sentiment by putting the Shakhty engineers on trial for 'wrecking'. However, the regime gave its full backing to management efforts to raise productivity by cutting piece rates, increasing output norms, as well as in the longer term introducing greater mechanization, standardization, and specialization of production. To encourage rationalization, time-study bureaux were set up and an army of psychophysiologists, psychotechnicians, and labour hygienists descended on the factories. Achievement fell well short of aspiration; yet by 1927 average hourly labour productivity had risen to a level 10% higher than in 1913.

Much of the rationalization drive was inspired by the 'scientific organization of labour', known by its Russian acronym NOT, an adaptation of F. W. Taylor's theory of 'scientific management'. This was one of the more egregious expressions of the 'productivist' strain within Bolshevism that perceived the social organization of labour inherited from capitalism, with its particular productivity techniques and technologies, to be perfectly compatible with socialism. One of its chief proponents, A. K. Gastev, a former syndicalist and 'worker-poet', ran the Central Institute of Labour from 1920: 'In the social sphere we must enter the epoch of precise measurement, formulae, blueprints, controlled calibration, social norms.' Gastev's dream of a socialist society in which man and machine would merge did not go unchallenged. When he proclaimed in *Pravda* in 1928 that 'the time has gone beyond recall when one could speak of the freedom of the worker in regard to the machine', critics in the Komsomol (Communist Youth League) said that his understanding of the worker was indistinguishable from that of Henry Ford. In the late 1920s, the impulse to make science the arbiter of industrial relations came increasingly into conflict with a different strain in Bolshevism, the heroic, voluntarist strain that stressed revolutionary will and collective initiative as the means to overcome Russia's backwardness. As early as 1926 'shock brigades' in the Ukrainian metallurgical industry and the Triangle rubber works in Leningrad set out to bust production norms, but 'socialist competition' and 'storming' did not become entrenched until the First Five-Year Plan.

In key respects workers' lives improved during the 1920s. Nowhere was this truer than with respect to the eight-hour working day. Real wages struggled to reach their pre-war level, but subsidized rents and transport meant that most workers were slightly better off. Women's wages rose relative to the pre-war period, partly because the Soviet Union became the first country in the world to introduce equal pay, but in 1928 their daily earnings were still only two-thirds those of men. Some 9 million trade-unionists enjoyed free medical care, maternity benefit, and disability and other pensions, although their real value remained pitifully low. By 1927 workers were eating somewhat better – consumption of meat, dairy products, and sugar had risen – although nutritional data suggest that diet had not improved since the 1890s. The number in employment rose substantially, to reach well over 10 million by 1929, but unemployment also rose, affecting women workers in particular. Initially, the rise in the number of jobless was due to demobilization of the Red Army and lay-offs provoked by a 'regime of economy' in industry; but later the rise was due to the resumption of peasant migration to the cities. In 1928 over a million people settled permanently in the cities, in addition to 3.9 million seasonal migrants, putting housing and rudimentary social services under extreme strain.

In the course of the 1920s work stoppages became fewer, shorter, and smaller in scope. According to official figures, strikes peaked in 1922 and 1923 but then fell steadily, dropping sharply in 1928. Given that working and living conditions remained very stressful, one might have expected the level of stoppages to have remained high, especially given the return to industry of many skilled and experienced workers. By 1929 half of all workers had started work before 1917. But the fall in strikes suggests not that workers were becoming less discontented, but that the regime was having some success in channelling their grievances through the rates-and-conflict commissions. Rising unemployment was doubtless also a factor depressing the level of stoppages. More generally, however, the fall in strikes may have been linked to a general increase in worker passivity that was of concern to the authorities. By 1925 the turn-out for elections to factory committees had fallen so low that the local party and trade-union cells were urged to ensure that the forthcoming elections were genuinely democratic. The campaign paid off since the numbers attending election meetings rose and in some areas as many as half the members elected to factory committees were non-party. But such signs of worker independence were always worrying to local authorities who soon resumed the habit of removing 'trouble makers'. By 1927 complaints of worker apathy were once again rife.

It is not easy to generalize about workers' political attitudes. The majority remained dissatisfied with their lot in spite of the fact that conditions had eased enormously compared with the civil war. However, even as they blamed the regime for their poor working and living conditions, they appear to have maintained faith with the Soviet ideal. A sample of 922 letters from urban correspondents (obviously a broader group than workers), intercepted by the Cheka in 1924–5, shows that 53% were favourably disposed towards soviet power – a lower percentage than among rural correspondents – but that 93% expressed dissatisfaction with the local authorities. In spring 1926 non-party worker conferences in Moscow voiced sharp criticism at the gap between workers' wages and those of white-collar employees, at stressful working conditions and dismal living conditions, and at the privileges enjoyed by the 'new masters': 'Lunacharsky's wife has diamond rings on her fingers and a gold necklace. Where has she got them from?' Such sentiment was rooted in a commitment to equality and collectivism, but it should not be idealized, since it could take on a reactionary hue, modulating easily into condemnations of 'Jews' – an amorphous 'other', readily associated with 'nepmen' (traders, manufacturers, and suppliers), Communist officials, and factory bosses. Nor should one forget that there was a sizeable contingent of workers who were deeply antipathetic to the regime; not because they considered it to have betrayed socialism, but because they resented its constant exhortations that they should repair their 'backward' ways, by abandoning drunkenness, male chauvinism, anti-semitism, and the like. Overall, however, the majority of workers appear to have been disappointed at the slow progress to socialism, blaming the regime for the gap between aspiration and reality. Yet the fact that they condemned it in terms of the ideals it claimed to uphold suggests that they still retained a belief in socialism and soviet power.

The inner-party struggle

In May 1922 Lenin suffered partial paralysis, severely undermining his capacity for work until October; in December he suffered two further strokes. Skirmishing within the party oligarchy to determine who should succeed him commenced, as the so-called triumvirate of Zinoviev, Stalin, and Kamenev emerged as the controlling group within the Politburo. In April 1922 Lenin's admiration of Stalin's skills as an administrator led to his being made the party's general secretary; before the year was out, he was expressing concern about the Stalin's behaviour. In December he wrote a testament in which he compared in somewhat begrudging terms the qualities of six members of the oligarchy. He reserved his harshest criticism for Stalin, whom he deemed rude, intolerant, and capricious, and urged that he be removed from his post as general secretary. He praised Trotsky for his outstanding abilities, yet chided him for his excessive self-assurance and preoccupation with administrative matters. Lenin's intention was that the testament should remain secret; but his secretary vouchsafed its contents to Stalin, who henceforward kept Lenin incommunicado, under the surveillance of doctors who reported to him alone. Despite his frailty, Lenin struggled to thwart Stalin's pretensions, objecting vigorously to the way he rode roughshod over the Georgian communists who dared to oppose his plan to absorb Georgia into the RSFSR. When on 4 March 1923 he learnt of an incident in which Stalin had subjected Krupskaia to a 'storm of coarse abuse', he fired off a furious letter threatening to break off relations with the general secretary. But his struggle against the 'marvellous Georgian' whom he had done so much to promote, though heroic, had come too late. On 10 March he suffered a massive stroke that left him speechless and paralysed, and in January 1924 he died.

15. Krupskaia and Lenin, Gorki, 1922

Trotsky was by far the most charismatic of Lenin's heirs yet he was heartily detested by the triumvirate. Not least of the factors that prevented him from stepping into Lenin's shoes was what A. Lunacharsky called 'his tremendous imperiousness and inability or unwillingness to be at all amiable and attentive to people'. Not until October 1923, against the background of the 'scissors crisis', did he come out in opposition to the triumvirate, lambasting the bureaucratization of the party and calling for accelerated industrialization in order to strengthen the proletariat. During 1924 Stalin and Zinoviev waged a vituperative campaign against this left opposition, impugning Trotsky's claim to be a Bolshevik by drawing attention to his conflicts with Lenin prior to 1917. Since Trotsky had been no friend to earlier opposition groups, his belated conversion to the cause of inner-party democracy was seen by many as no more than a cover for 'bonapartist' ambitions.

In late 1924, to counter the left's claim that international revolution was the sole means of guaranteeing Russia's survival as a socialist regime, Stalin enunciated a new doctrine of 'socialism in one country', thereby inaugurating a process that would end in the 1930s in the full-scale rehabilitation of Russia's history and traditions. Once Trotsky had been removed from the presidency of the Revolutionary Military Council in January 1925, Zinoviev and Kamenev turned their fire on Bukharin, the most eloquent defender of NEP. They believed that excessive concessions were now being made to the peasantry and knew that Stalin, about whose ambitions they had been concerned for a long time, stood full-square behind Bukharin. At the Fourteenth Party Congress in December 1925, they attacked the general secretary's vast concentration of power, but Stalin was by now powerful enough to have them removed from key positions. In summer 1926, in an astonishing turn of events, Zinoviev and Kamenev joined forces with their erstwhile foe, Trotsky, to form the United Opposition. Stalin, determined to annihilate this new challenge, aligned himself with a right-wing bloc of Bukharin, A. Rykov, head of the Council of People's Commissars, and

Tomsky, the trade-union leader. In October 1926 Trotsky and Zinoviev were hounded from the Central Committee, accused of representing a 'social democratic deviation', and by November 1927 both had been expelled from the party. In January 1928 Trotsky was exiled to Alma Ata, a prelude to his deportation and ultimate assassination at the hands of Stalin's henchmen. As the grain procurement crisis deepened in 1927–8, however, Stalin shifted position decisively. Spurning the gradualism favoured by the right, he called in 1928 for a 'decisive struggle' against 'right opportunism'. Brilliant theoretician though he was, Bukharin was no match for him politically. By April 1929 the 'right opposition', which barely functioned as an organized faction, was smashed and Bukharin expelled from the Politburo.

At the heart of the inner-party struggle was a conflict about the optimal strategy for industrializing Russia in conditions of economic and social backwardness and international isolation. Yet the central place of class within Bolshevik ideology meant that the debate focused less on technical questions than on whether particular policies were 'proletarian' or 'bourgeois' in their implications. Trotsky accepted the framework of NEP – the market, material incentives, and the alliance with the peasantry – but emphasized the primacy of building state industry and defending the proletariat. Bukharin, by contrast, argued that the preservation of the alliance with the peasantry was the overriding priority. Peasants should be allowed to prosper – thus his slogan 'Enrich yourselves', which so outraged the left – since the more efficient state sector would meet the rising demand for consumer goods, gradually squeezing out the private sector. Bukharin recognized that progress would be slow, likening his programme to 'riding into socialism on a peasant nag', but the United Opposition was alarmed because they believed that this would allow 'kulak' forces to strengthen. So long as NEP appeared to be working, Stalin pursued a middle course, successfully exploiting divisions among his opponents. In 1926 he inclined to the right rather than to the left, opposing the Dnieprostroi dam on the grounds that it was like a peasant buying a gramophone when he should be repairing his plough. But as the perception gained ground that NEP was running into the sand, he switched course sharply, demanding by 1928 a pace of industrialization far more hectic than anything ever contemplated by the left. Since the country was falling ever further behind the advanced capitalist powers, the Stalin faction insisted that speed was of the essence and that a decisive breakthrough could come about only by breaking with NEP.

Although one cannot interpret the inner-party conflict as a naked struggle for power, the issue of power was nevertheless at its heart. Lenin, who had ruled by virtue of his charisma rather than formal position, bequeathed a structure of weak but bloated institutions that relied for direction on a strong leader. No one in the oligarchy enjoyed anything like his personal authority. The question of who should succeed him thus raised thorny issues about the institutionalization of power. Though hardly champions of socialist democracy, the left opposition stood for collective leadership, against the extreme concentration of power in the central organs of the party, and for tolerance of a range of opinion within the party. Yet they believed in the paramount importance of discipline and unity and were terrified of being seen as splitters. This disarmed them psychologically – no more pathetic evidence for which exists than Trotsky's admission to the Thirteenth Party Congress in May 1924 that 'the party in the last analysis is always right.' Stalin ably traded on the widespread fear of disunity, building up a reputation as a champion of orthodoxy against assorted malcontents. By harping on Trotsky's differences with Lenin in the past, he attached himself to the growing cult of Lenin, notably with the publication in 1924 of his *Foundations of Leninism*, which set up Lenin as the touchstone of political rectitude. This became a key text in the education of the tens of thousands of new recruits who were easily persuaded that the 'anti-Leninism' of the opposition deprived them of the right to a fair hearing. Similarly, by nailing his colours to the mast of 'socialism in one country', Stalin opened up the positive perspective of backward Russia raising herself through her own efforts, without waiting for international revolution. Trotsky, against whom the new doctrine was targeted, never in fact denied that it was possible to begin socialist construction; but he saw international revolution as necessary in the longer term if Russia were not to be forced into autarchy and diplomatic isolation. Stalin characterized Trotsky's perspective of permanent revolution as one of 'permanent gloom' and 'permanent hopelessness'. He and his supporters, by contrast, presented themselves as optimistic, loyal and disciplined, 'doers' rather than whiners. This played to the latent nationalism in the burgeoning ranks of young party members, mostly working-class, who whilst parroting the language of class and internationalism, deeply resented the notion that Russia was inferior to the West.

> Dear Comrade Leaders
>
> I am writing you a letter because I want to tell you what impression is being made on us, the dark, undeveloped, backward people, by the case of comrade Zinoviev and other of our officials. Comrades, as a backward, dark fellow, I cannot imagine the construction of socialism without tight cohesion of our party and leadership. I fully understand what will happen if at the heart of the construction of socialism are quarrelling, lack of coordination, disunity. We will build nothing. And how will the bourgeoisie and the western countries look on us? They will make fun of us, they will listen open-mouthed, expecting the break-up of our soviet power. If there are quarrels this will once again make it easier for provocateurs and Mensheviks to spread their lying propaganda against soviet power. I am a young worker who was born in 1902 and who joined the Komsomol in 1923.
>
> Letter from P. Ivanov, a worker, to the Central Committee
> Vyshchi Ol'chedaevskii works, Nemirch station, Mogilev district,
> Podol'sk province

This ideological and psychological context helps us to understand why Stalin came out on top in the inner-party conflict; but it hardly explains how an able but relatively inconspicuous 'organization man' could become one of the 20th century's most savage tyrants. To appreciate this, one must look to Stalin's personality and to his brilliant grasp of machine politics. Stalin, in contrast to Lenin and Trotsky, was born into poverty, into a family where his violent and drunken father was frequently absent. This early experience bred a deeply pessimistic outlook on life; he shared completely the view of Machiavelli – whom he had read – that 'men are ungrateful, fickle, liars and deceivers'. Outshone intellectually by the likes of Trotsky and Kamenev, he made his mark by his immense capacity for detailed work. A first-rate tactician with an excellent memory, he was cool and calculating, averse to the histrionics to which Zinoviev and Trotsky were prone. In the words of M. I. Riutin, leader of the last of the opposition groupings in the early 1930s, he was 'narrow-minded, sly, power-loving, vengeful, treacherous, envious, hypocritical, insolent, boastful, stubborn'. What this misses is the fact that he was also genial and unstuffy, with a capacity to make himself agreeable.

From April 1922 Stalin was the only member of the oligarchy who was simultaneously a full member of the Politburo, the Orgburo, and the Secretariat. Through control of the latter two organs, he was able to influence the agenda of the Politburo and to determine the appointment of personnel down to local district party secretaries. One of his first acts as general secretary was to order the latter to report to him personally by the fifth of each month. Gradually, he used his patronage to appoint supporters to key positions in the party-state apparatus and to break up the power bases of his opponents, including Zinoviev's stronghold in Leningrad and Uglanov's rightist base in Moscow. At each of the key turning-points in the inner-party struggle, with the exception of the battle against the 'rightist deviation' in 1928, most lower-level party leaders swung behind Stalin. By 1929 the 'moustachioed one' had acquired absolute control over the party machine, turning the Secretariat into his personal chancery and revealing a positively byzantine capacity for intrigue and subterfuge.

Party and people

During the 1920s a new ruling elite began to emerge, defined by its privileges and powerful political connections. The key mechanism through which it was constituted was the 'nomenklatura' system, established in 1920, whereby the Central Committee (or the relevant provincial or district committee in the case of junior positions) reserved to itself the right to make key appointments in party and state administration. By 1922 the personnel assignment office of the Central Committee was responsible for over 10,000 appointments nation-wide. The emergent elite consisted of party officials at *oblast'* (provincial) level and above, senior state officials, and leading industrial managers. In 1927 there were about 3,000 to 4,000 higher party officials and about 100,000 at middle and lower levels. When one adds senior officials in the state apparatus, including industry and education, perhaps half a million people – out of a working population of more than 86 million – may be said to have formed this elite. By a decision of the Twelfth Party Conference in August 1922, responsible officials down to the level of district party secretaries were guaranteed rations, housing, uniforms, health care, and rest cures in the Crimea. Family members also enjoyed these privileges. However, in contrast to their counterparts in capitalist countries, members of the elite derived power and privilege from tenure of office, rather than ownership of property and wealth, and they enjoyed no security of tenure and were unable to bequeath their office to their offspring.

Between 1921 and 1929 party membership roughly doubled, to reach over a million, in spite of a series of 'purges' – a term that had not yet acquired a sinister ring – to remove hundreds of thousands of members for passivity, careerism, or drunkenness. The party succeeded in 'proletarianizing' itself, insofar as by 1927 nearly half its members were workers by social origin. Over 300,000 of these 'workers', however, were actually occupied in white-collar or administrative positions. As this expansion took place, 'Old Bolsheviks' went into eclipse. In 1925 only 2,000 members had joined the party before 1905. Many of these were intellectuals, who had suffered imprisonment and internal exile or lived for periods abroad, whose values were very different from those of plebeian incomers. Most of the incomers had only primary education and little grasp of Marxist theory. In the mid-1920s the party control commission found that 72% of party members in Voronezh were 'politically illiterate'. Though doubtless sincere, they understood building socialism largely as entailing the conscientious performance of tasks set down by the leadership. Moreover, as secret police reports regularly commented, not least of their motivations was the desire 'to get a higher-paying job and a good apartment'. Those plebeians promoted into administrative positions – and in Votskaia autonomous region (formerly part of Viatka province) they constituted no less than half the party membership – saw their promotion as proof that the proletariat was now the ruling class, although probably no more than 5% of the total workforce ever benefited from such upward mobility.

Meanwhile the 'bureaucratization' of the party continued apace. In his last years, perhaps under the strain of illness, Lenin's writings took on a dark, pessimistic tone. 'We are being sucked into a foul, bureaucratic swamp.' Yet he continued to believe that the solution lay in promoting workers and in getting the Workers and Peasants' Inspectorate (Rabkrin) and the party control commission to wage war on inefficiency and inertia in the state and party respectively. These new agencies, however, rapidly succumbed to the disease they were meant to cure. In Tver' no less than 29 different sections of Rabkrin carried out an inspection of the local textile industry. The 1920s saw endless appeals to activists to expose corruption, incompetence, and capriciousness, but there was little awareness that 'bureaucratism' was a systemic rather than an individual problem. At the same time, despite the proliferating division of labour, the ramified hierarchies, and the ever-lengthening trail of paperwork, the operation of power was not strictly 'bureaucratic' at all. For the system relied far more on personalized authority than on formal institutions and procedures. Middle- and lower-level officials, with little security of tenure or institutional protection against superiors, developed networks of clients to consolidate their influence in their particular sphere and to protect themselves against the centre. Behind the facade of bureaucratic hierarchy, power was frequently transacted through 'family influence', with local bosses, such as G. K. Ordzhonikidze in Tbilisi, Kirov in Baku, or F. I. Goloshchekin in Kazakhstan, presiding over extensive personal fiefdoms.

One key difference that marked the period of NEP out from both the civil war and the 1930s was the abandonment of terror as an instrument of political rule. The secret police was not eliminated, but the OGPU, which replaced the Cheka, confined itself to routine surveillance of the population and to external state security. More importantly, a conscious effort was made to broaden the scope of law. In 1922 a Criminal Code was enacted, that drew to a surprising degree on elements of tsarist jurisprudence. A centralized court system re-emerged and the office of procurator soon became the most powerful judicial agency. The practice of law was once again professionalized; but trained lawyers remained thin on the ground, so lay judges and assessors, poorly paid and dependent on the good will of officials, continued to be influential. Many of the values of the revolution, moreover, continued to influence judicial practice, so that criminals from the 'toiling classes' – especially juvenile offenders, among whom there was an explosion in crime – continued to be treated with marked leniency and with a strong emphasis on rehabilitation. Nevertheless there were clear limits to the institutionalization of a law-bound society: the judiciary failed to develop meaningful independence from the state and certainly failed to protect the individual against the state. Moreover, the Bolsheviks, in continuing to see law principally as a means of defending the state, unconsciously served as perpetuators of Russian tradition.

The countryside remained as under-governed as in the tsarist period: indeed the ratio of police to population was actually lower than before 1917. Party control was secure only down to the level of the county executives of the soviets, although during the 1920s rapid headway was made in bolstering party control of township executives. In the village soviets the party's influence was negligible. Even by 1928 there was only one party organization for every 26 rural centres of population. Peasants took some interest in the village soviets and township executives, since these influenced the allocation of taxes and land; but they were generally indifferent to the county soviets: 'We have no objection to government; we need authority, but we don't care how it's organized.' Barely a quarter of members of county executives were peasants, compared with 44% who were 'employees', most of whom had formerly worked for the zemstvos. The members of the township executives and village soviets, by contrast, consisted overwhelmingly of peasants, generally but not always drawn from the poorer strata. The 'youth who doesn't yet shave', with a record of service in the Red Army and limited primary education, was the archetypal representative of the rural soviets. Despite efforts to increase female representation in the village soviets, this only rose from 1% in 1922 to 12% by 1927. The personnel in the lower soviets did not command much respect, partly because they were seen by older villagers as callow and ignorant of farming, partly because they compensated for their poor salaries with corruption and embezzlement. Complaints against them were legion. Nevertheless peasants also comment on the absence of 'nobs' in local government and on the fact that the soviets were led by 'our people whom we can scold and have a cigarette with', which suggests that the boundary between state and society had become more porous since the tsarist period.

At the start of NEP the profound alienation of the peasants from the regime was reflected in the fact that only 22% of rural voters (and only 14% of women) took part in the soviet elections of 1922. The 'Face to the Countryside' campaign of autumn 1924 sought to revitalize rural soviets, exhorting them to be 'polite, attentive, listening to the voice of the peasantry', with the result that participation rose to 47% in 1926–7. In the unprecedentedly free election of 1925, communists were voted out of soviets in some areas and there were widespread calls for the establishment of peasant unions. The increased assertiveness of the peasantry made the regime uneasy, fuelling anxiety about the kulak threat. It is foolhardy to generalize about the political attitudes of 100 million peasants, except to say that they were far from being a cowed mass. Moreover, in spite of its fears about kulaks, the regime encouraged them to speak out. With some certainty, one can say that enthusiastic supporters of the regime were in a minority, as were its implacable foes. The majority in between probably considered authority in any form oppressive and no doubt felt that the revolution had changed little in the way that government acted upon the governed. Nevertheless tension between peasants and government eased after 1923. A sample of 407 letters from peasants to Red Army soldiers, intercepted by military censors between 1924 and 1925, shows that almost two-thirds were positively disposed to the soviet government – probably a peak figure – but that virtually all were critical of local authorities. Analysis of letters sent to the *Peasant Newspaper* between 1924 and 1928 suggests that the key concerns – after taxation – were the price and quality of manufactures, fleecing by middlemen, exploitation by kulaks, the eight-hour day enjoyed by workers, and the better cultural provision in the towns. Many of these issues reflect a deep sense that peasants were second-class citizens in the new order. In 1926 for the first time more correspondents (28%) expressed dissatisfaction with soviet power than support (23%). The gist of most letters was that the majority of peasants live in great hardship ('unshod and unclothed', 'puffed up with hunger') due to taxes and rigged prices. Many forthrightly blamed the government. One letter from 100 poor peasants inveighed: 'Communists and commissars, you have all forgotten 1917. You parasites sit in your warm berths drinking our blood.' It appears that millions had begun to internalize the language of the regime, to take at face value its claims to be building socialism. By

Esteemed Mikhail Ivanovich!

I send you greetings from the distant and poor Kirghiz autonomous oblast, greetings from a peasant woman from the Samara steppe. I am writing to you only because you also are a peasant and a worker and at present are the defender and mediator of the poor. Mikhail Ivanovich, we struggled, much blood was spilt, many innocent people perished. They fought for social equality. But where is it? I have seen in our proletarian country, alongside terrifying luxury, even more terrifying poverty. Once again I feel hatred in my breast, as I did in the past, but then I knew at whom to direct my hatred and in whose downfall to rejoice. Our financial director receives 140 rubles a month, plus a furnished apartment with lighting and heating. But the caretaker who has to stoke six boilers each day, cart 12 puds of fuel, carry water on her shoulders so that staff can wash their hands, she receives 12 rubles, has no work clothes, no day off, and no holidays. I have quarrelled with some who call themselves party members, but all they can say in answer to my questions is that it's impossible to make everyone equal. There are some who are clever and some who are fools. But I heard all that under Nicholas. When I was a child I would spend sleepless nights wanting to express my thoughts to that dear old man, Lev Nikolaevich Tolstoy, but I didn't have the courage to write to him and in any case it was dangerous. Now I am 34 and have three children and am almost an invalid, but am still as anxious as before.

K. I. Tokareva to M. I. Kalinin, 9 March 1926, Town Hospital,
Urda Bukeevskaia

no stretch of the imagination did this mean that they felt satisfied: indeed the gap between Soviet ideal and quotidian reality probably intensified their disillusionment in a government that fell so short of its own standards. Yet in criticizing the regime for failing to live up to its ideals, they implicitly ascribed a certain legitimacy to it.

Nation-building

The idea of a Union of Soviet Socialist Republics, in which the RSFSR would be one republic among several, was not formalized until 1922. By that date, a series of bilateral treaties between the RSFSR and the republics of Ukraine, Belorussia, Georgia, Armenia, Azerbaijan, Bukhara, Khorezm, and the Far East had begun to cement these states into a federation. C. Rakovsky, the Bulgarian head of the Ukrainian soviet government, and the Georgian Bolsheviks, P. G. Mdivani and F. I. Makharadze, favoured a loose arrangement whereby republics would remain sovereign entities. By contrast, Stalin favoured 'autonomization', which entailed incorporating the republics into the RSFSR. Lenin rejected this solution as redolent of the chauvinism of the old regime, and insisted on a federation in which non-Russian republics would have equal status with the RSFSR. Stalin was forced to accept this, but took advantage of Lenin's illness to ensure that the devolution of power to non-Russian republics did not weaken the party's dictatorship. The constitution of the USSR, finally ratified on 31 January 1924, left no doubt that ultimate power lay with Moscow. Where non-Russians resisted incorporation, they were duly crushed, as in summer 1925 when I. S. Unshlikht led 7,000 troops, including 8 planes and 22 heavy artillery, to 'disarm the bandit population' of Chechnia.

Nevertheless within the framework of a Russian-dominated Soviet Union, the 1920s witnessed an extraordinary process of nation-building, as the Bolsheviks entrenched nationality as the major principle of socio-political organization. Ethnographers set to work classifying ethnic groups, many of which had little understanding of themselves as nations, and programmes were devised to promote native political elites and intelligentsias together with minority languages and cultures. The process was designed, in Stalin's words, to produce republics and autonomous regions that were 'national in form, but socialist in content'. This was something of a paradox, since the Soviet Union claimed to represent the transcendence of the nation-state and, at various times, deployed a rhetoric of ultimate 'fusion' of nations into a single Soviet people. In practice, however, nationality, once seen as an impediment to socialism, came to be viewed positively – as the modality through which the economic, political, and cultural development of the non-Russian peoples would take place. Having eliminated traditional elites, the regime created a base for itself in the non-Russian republics by promoting members of the indigenous population – mainly young, politically active males from humble backgrounds – to positions of leadership. By institutionalizing the autonomies as political units and by creating national elites, Soviet rule helped to create quasi-nations, albeit at sub-state level. Broadly, this policy of indigenizing the party-state was vindicated. The proportion of Ukrainians in the Ukrainian Communist Party, for example, rose from 24% in 1922 to 52% in 1927, while Kazakh membership of that republic's party grew from 8% to 53% between 1924 and 1933. At the centre, however, Slavs continued to monopolize the key positions in the political, military, and security apparatuses. In other words, the limits of autonomy were firmly set by Moscow and those who dared to buck those limits risked the fate of the talented Sultangaliev, who was tried in June 1923 for being a 'national communist'.

The cultural dimension of the programme of nation-building, which took the form of mass literacy and education and the promotion of print culture in native languages, was a brilliant success. Alphabets were devised for people who had no written language. By 1927, 82% of schools in Ukraine were teaching through the medium of Ukrainian. Native intelligentsias were offered preferential access to higher education and professional positions. Where there were minority peoples within national autonomies they were given their own national soviets. In the Far East, for example, Chinese and Korean peoples enjoyed an unprecedented degree of tolerance, taking part in local government, establishing their own schools and newspapers. This emphasis on cultural-national autonomy, however, did not preclude conflict. The Tatars favoured updating Arabic as the written medium of their language, whereas Muslims in Azerbaijan and the northern Caucasus pressed for a Latin script. By 1925 official opinion had lined up behind the latter. Moscow genuinely encouraged national diversity, but always on its terms. Firmly committed to an evolutionist view of social development, it did not consider all cultures equal and had little compunction in attacking aspects of cultures, such as those in Central Asia, which it deemed 'backward'. Indeed one's very recognition as a nation depended on Moscow: the Kurds, for example, were never so recognized; and the extent of one's political autonomy was also dependent on the whim of Moscow, Abkhazia, for example, had its full republican status withdrawn in 1931. The 1920s, then, were a unique era of nation-building, yet contradictions between the institutionalization of nationality within a federal structure and the centralization of economic and political power in a Slav-dominated unitary state were evident from the first.

Crisis of NEP

Between 1926–7 and 1928–9 the terms of trade for agriculture improved, owing to a lowering of industrial prices; but though the total volume of food sold continued to rise, grain sales did not increase. Indeed a lowering of the procurement price of grain led to a serious shortage by the autumn of 1927, when only 16.9% of the harvest was marketed. By the summer of 1928 rationing had been reintroduced in the cities. Meanwhile, the government was committed to stepping up the rate of investment in heavy industry, a commitment hardened by the war scare of summer 1927, brought on by Britain's severance of diplomatic relations. The procurement crisis of 1928 thus threw into doubt whether the ambitious targets of the First Five-Year Plan, ratified in December 1927, could be realized. Many in the party were now convinced that kulaks were holding the country to ransom. Having trounced the right opposition, Stalin resolved to smash these 'bourgeois' forces.

In recent years NEP has been the subject of heated debate. During Gorbachev's perestroika from 1986 to 1991, many argued that NEP could have delivered balanced economic growth at a rate equal to that achieved by the crash industrialization of the First Five-Year Plan, once allowance is made for waste and destruction. With the collapse of the Soviet Union in 1991, the consensus changed, historians arguing that NEP was doomed to collapse under the weight of its contradictions. The foregoing account has tried to show that whilst where is no absolute contradiction between plan and market, NEP was a deeply contradictory system. From the start it proved vulnerable to crises, and as it evolved the temptation to use command-administrative methods to alter the workings of the market proved irresistible. Yet in 1928 NEP was not in terminal crisis. Grain procurement was a serious problem, springing directly from the strategy of prioritizing investment in heavy industry in an economy where there was an acute shortage of consumer goods, but a change in the price of grain relative to other agricultural commodities could have improved grain sales. The key problem was that NEP could not generate the level of investment required to sustain the rate of industrialization to which Stalin and his epigones were now committed. Ludicrously ambitious though their targets for growth subsequently became, they were not necessarily wrong to think that growth had to be rapid. In particular, the tense international situation created by the Versailles peace settlement left the Soviet Union vulnerable to hostile powers, and dictated that she build her economic and military strength as rapidly as possible.

Nevertheless, in the final instance, the break with NEP was determined not by sober assessment of the international situation or by technical discussion of rates of investment, but by ideology. One may doubt that kulaks were gaining ground on the proletariat, but Bolsheviks, like everyone else, acted not upon the basis of 'reality' but upon their perception of reality. The party's entire rationale was to bring about 'socialism'; now it looked as though the continuance of NEP would cause the state to drown in a sea of petty-bourgeois forces or succumb to international capital. However, if the deep structure of Bolshevik ideology – its calculus of class forces – made the break with NEP likely, it did not mean that ideology necessitated the violent 'dekulakization', wildly escalating planning targets, the terror, and forced labour that Stalin proceeded to unleash. The choice to go on an all-out 'offensive' was precisely that: a choice made by Stalin and his supporters.

With NEP the meaning of the revolution changed profoundly: it was no longer principally about equality, justice, popular power, or internationalism, but about the party-state mobilizing the country's human and material resources to overcome economic, social, and cultural backwardness as rapidly as possible. As the Bolsheviks themselves recognized, the options were now heavily circumscribed by international isolation and by a backward economy and social structure. It should also be added that their options were circumscribed by the institutions and practices of the party-state that were now in place, although they were less capable of appreciating this. In this context, the project of proletarian self-emancipation gave way to one of exploiting the productive power of the proletariat and peasantry in order to drag the country out of backwardness. As this happened, Bolshevik ideology mutated, with more elitist and technocratic tendencies coming to prevail, at least for the time being. It was in this limiting structural context that the inner party struggle was played out.

Lenin bequeathed a structure of power that rested on personalized leadership, making the individual qualities of the leader of far more consequence than is the case for leaders in democratic states. The struggle to find a successor to Lenin, and the ideological conflicts bound up with that struggle, were thus fraught with consequence for the future course of the revolution. The death of Lenin at the age of 53 was a fateful contingency, not least because he had become convinced that Stalin posed a threat to party unity. Had he lived, he could probably have nipped in the bud the ambitions of a man whom he had done much to promote. Moreover, notwithstanding the narrowing of revolutionary options or the narrowing of the permitted debate within the party, Bolshevism still retained some ideological diversity. Lenin had begun to reflect on the implications for socialism of Russia's backwardness and isolation. It was on these rather sketchy reflections that Bukharin built his model of NEP, one in which the state and private sectors would interact through the market and in which civil peace would be the paramount goal of the party. A very different scenario was offered by the Left, in which industrialization would proceed robustly at the expense of the peasantry until revolution broke out in the more developed world. There were, in other words, real choices to be made. But one should not, finally, lose sight of the fact that these choices were fundamentally circumscribed by the exigencies of backwardness and international isolation. One may speculate that Bukharin's socialism at a snail's pace would have gradually eroded the party's monopoly of power and allowed the economic and military gap between the Soviet Union and the capitalist powers to widen. Similarly, Trotsky's hope that Russia could be saved by revolution in the West proved vain. Notwithstanding the acute instability of world capitalism after 1929, or the rise of fascism, no western country experienced the systemic breakdown that constitutes a true revolutionary situation, i.e. one in which revolutionaries have a real chance of taking power. In the absence of revolution in the capitalist West, it is unlikely that the Left could have avoided some form of coercion in its bid to industrialize, since the capacity of the peasant to thwart the goals of the regime was considerable and coercion was built into the very structure of the relationship between state and society. Use of coercion, however, does not imply the Great Terror. It was Stalin who recognized that the totalitarian state could be used to smash the constraints of backwardness through a 'revolution from above'. He did not scruple at the cost.

Chapter 5
NEP: society and culture

With the onset of NEP social inequality began to increase. Class remained a fragile structure, since its material underpinnings such as ownership of means of production, the employment of labour, and the exercise of managerial authority were weak. Moreover, there were plenty of opportunities to advance oneself – by leaving the village, by getting an education, by joining the Komsomol, by getting a job in a soviet institution – so social relations remained fluid. Compared with capitalist societies, Soviet society was not highly differentiated, yet its pattern of differentiation was more complex than official categories allowed. Leaving aside the emerging nomenklatura elite, which not surprisingly was absent from official categories, the most rapidly growing occupational group were the service employees, a heterogeneous category, which embraced hundreds of thousands of office workers and petty functionaries in the state and party apparatuses, clerical, managerial, and technical staff in industry, and unskilled workers in the service sector. By 1926 they constituted the largest occupational group in Moscow. In strict Marxist terms, these were an unproductive stratum that formed part of the petty-bourgeoisie. Faced by the seemingly spontaneous proliferation of social groups that had no place in the idealized model of socialism, the Bolsheviks struggled to control the confusing social world of NEP by imposing familiar categories of class upon it.

The Bolsheviks were convinced that differentiation was increasing among the peasantry. The recovery of the rural population had been rapid. By 1926, 82% of the 147 million people in the Soviet Union – 5.5% higher than in 1914 – lived in the countryside. The number of peasant households was rising fast – from 18.7 million in 1914 to about 24 million in 1927 – owing to the desire of sons to split from the parental household. In spite of these tendencies, the great bulk of peasant households were classed as middle peasants, since they worked principally for subsistence and relied on their own labour. The Bolsheviks, however, were convinced that NEP was increasing the number of rich and poor households at the expense of those in the middle. This is how they interpreted statistics such as those which purported to show that in 1927 26% of households were poor; that 57% belonged to the 'middle' peasantry; 14% to the 'upper middle'; and 3.2% to the kulaks. These statistics classified households according to the value of their 'means of production', but the extent of differentiation varied according to the means of production one looked at. Sown area per capita, for example, was distributed fairly equally; holdings of livestock, rented land, and hired labour were distributed less equally; and ownership of machinery was distributed very unequally. Moreover if one measured the data by household rather than per capita the degree of differentiation became greater. The real concern of the Bolsheviks was with what they believed to be the growing influence of kulaks. Of all categories, none was harder to define than this. Formerly associated with money-lending, kulaks could be variously defined as wealthy farmers, especially if they hired labour; as farmers who produced mainly for the market; as farmers who hired out heavy machinery or draft animals; or as peasants whose wealth derived from trade in such items as liquor. It is probably reasonable to conclude that the degree of differentiation among the peasantry was greater than many western historians allow; but it is unlikely that kulaks were flourishing at the expense of the middle peasants, if only because full-blown NEP was in operation for too short a time.

If the regime was alarmed by the supposed increase in influence of kulaks, it was also greatly exercised by 'nepmen', i.e. the traders, manufacturers, and suppliers who seized the new opportunities to engage in private enterprise. Probably the biggest group of the 3 million so classified were engaged in handicrafts in the countryside, but it was those who traded or ran small businesses in the cities who came in for most obloquy, since some amassed considerable fortunes. There was surprisingly little overlap between them and the pre-revolutionary merchant class, except among the rarefied elite of large wholesalers. Among ordinary folk, struggling to feed and clothe themselves, traditional hatred of 'speculators' found a focus in the nepmen, some of it acquiring an anti-semitic tinge. Such antipathy was reinforced by the merciless caricature of nepmen in the official media as vulgar *nouveaux riches*, ignorant upstarts, swindlers, and philistines. In truth, many nepmen did flaunt their wealth, dining on caviar and champagne, hiring servants, buying houses, dressing in suits, silk dresses, or expensive fur coats. So far as the regime was concerned they existed on sufferance, necessary to revive a devastated market yet feared as polluters of the social body.

In an effort to master this threatening environment, the Bolsheviks classified society into 'exploiters/disenfranchised' – mainly, kulaks, nepmen, *spetsy* – and 'toilers', who comprised a hegemonic proletariat, the poor peasants and the less reliable middle peasants. Exploiters were deprived of the vote, penalized in terms of taxation, access to higher education and to housing, and barred from membership of the Komsomol or party. By 1927–8 the proportion of those deprived of the vote had risen to 7.7% in the towns and 3.5% in the countryside. From 1928 military service was made compulsory for all male toilers aged 19 to 40, but 'non-toilers' were not entrusted to defend the motherland, receiving a 'white ticket' and being required instead to enrol in the home guard and pay a large military tax. Compulsory military service thus reinforced a definition of citizenship in class as well as gendered terms. In practice class labels were applied fairly arbitrarily. Local soviets

16. Anti-capitalist demonstration, 1920s

might disenfranchize middle and even poor peasants for hiring nurses or workers during harvest time on the grounds that this rendered them exploiters. Members of religious sects or parish councils might be consigned to the ranks of the kulaks.

Insofar as the social structure was constituted in part by political mechanisms, the Bolshevik taxonomy bore a distinct resemblance to the tsarist system of social estates, rights and duties being ascribed to groups on the basis of their place in the politico-juridical order. Because one's categorization had material consequences for one's life chances – after 1928 the disenfranchized did not qualify for rations and were likely to be expelled from state housing – it made real claims on one's social identity. The many who appealed against disenfranchisement invariably made the point that they were workers and that any lapse into 'non-toiling activity' – i.e. trade – had been due to pressure of circumstances. 'I took up trade not for profit but to support my family.' Their appeals, moreover, attest to the regime's having a certain legitimacy, since even those who felt themselves unjustly treated appear to have believed that disenfranchizement was a legitimate means for weeding out of the system of distribution those who had become rich at the people's expense. Bolshevik ideology was thus far more than imposed illusion, despite the many contradictions between it and the lived experience of ordinary citizens.

All my life since the age of eight, when I was left a total orphan, I have striven to earn a crust of bread by doing the hard work of a domestic servant. Absolutely alone, illiterate, I have from my earliest childhood dragged out a pitiful existence as a worker. In 1917 I came as a refugee from Lithuania. Of course, I experienced what only someone without a single kopeck to their name endures. With great difficulty I got a job as a servant and remained there until 1919. Then I joined a Jewish kindergarten on the technical side. I lost my job when it shut down. Having barely a single acquaintance in Moscow, being completely alone and still not having mastered Russian, I was completely unable to find a permanent position. The labour exchange found temporary work for me several times. I worked as a day labourer, but to supplement my income I sold sunflower seeds and other bits and pieces for a time. When I began to earn more as a day labourer I gave up this trade. My health is now so broken that I can scarcely do the smallest amount of work and now suddenly I am put on a level with the bourgeoisie, with exploiters who have no understanding of such a dark proletarian life as mine.

Woman appealing against her loss of voting rights

Designing a welfare state

In addition to categorizing the population, the Soviet state sought to refashion it through education, health care, housing, urban planning, and social work. In its commitment to improve the welfare of its people, it may be seen as an authoritarian variant of the welfare states that were emerging in Europe in this period. Healthcare was an area where the Bolshevik record was particularly impressive, although marred by inequality. War and revolution had led to a drastic deterioration in health standards, evinced by the fact that the average height of male conscripts fell from 1.69 metres in 1908 to 1.66 metres in 1924. During the first decade of Bolshevik power, health facilities, personnel, and services improved, as did their management. Perhaps the most striking index of this was the sharp fall in the death rate. Overall, however, the quantity and quality of health services remained low and the peasantry seriously disadvantaged. The ratio of doctors to population rose significantly, yet in 1926 there was still only one doctor for every 18,900 of the rural population. Central to the policy of the health commissariat was a programme of preventive medicine – obligatory vaccination against smallpox was introduced – and health education. 'Sanitary-enlightenment' propaganda developed rapidly to combat disease and popular ignorance; campaigns such as that in the Red Army to 'Help the Country with a Toothbrush' were designed to convey the message that making one's life healthy was a sign of 'consciousness'. Another dimension of the drive to enhance the productive and reproductive power of socialist society lay in the official promotion of sport, something that had no parallel under the *ancien régime*. Trade unions and the Komsomol promoted team sports, although some saw these as 'bourgeois' – since they were competitive – favouring all-round fitness for the masses instead. Following party intervention in 1925, the emphasis was put on sport as a means of promoting health and fitness, clean living, rationality, group identification, and military training.

The Bolsheviks promised free primary and secondary education within a coeducational and comprehensive school system. Building on progressive educational theories influential in late-imperial Russia, Lunacharsky, Commissar of Enlightenment, and Krupskaia, Lenin's wife, promoted polytechnicism – the idea of an all-round education without vocational specialization – and the 'unified labour school' where pupils took part in vocational training as a way of familiarizing them with the world of work. Entrance examinations, grading, homework, and punishment were all abolished. Relations between the government and teachers got off to a bad start when teachers went on strike, and throughout the civil war most teachers remained hostile to principles of progressive, child-centred education. Significant strides were made in extending education: by 1926–7 eight out of ten children aged 8 to 11 were in school, compared with 49% in 1915. As against that, expenditure per pupil remained well below the pre-war level and as late as 1926 teachers earned less than half what they had earned in 1913. In a context where levels of educational achievement were still very low, the Komsomol and trade unions pressed for greater specialization and more vocational education. This was resisted by the commissariat of education until 1926 when it went some way to reinstate a more traditional curriculum. This was not sufficient to palliate critics, however, and in 1929 Lunacharsky was removed.

In 1918 a 'revolutionary housing repartition' was proclaimed under the slogan 'Peace to the Hovels, War to the Palaces'. Workers were moved from their 'cots' and 'corners' and placed in the apartments of the wealthy. So-called 'nobs'' (*barskie*) apartments, with their interconnecting rooms, high ceilings, huge stoves, kitchens, and lavatories, generally proved unsuitable for what were later known as *kommunalki*, or communal apartments where each family had a separate room but shared a kitchen, lavatory, and corridor. This made for much friction among their inhabitants. As Woland says in M. A. Bulgakov's novel, *Master and Margarita*: 'People are people. It's just the housing question that spoils them.' With NEP, 'housing repartition' was

17. Children's demonstration

ended and most property was returned to its former owners. In 1922 rents were reintroduced, but consumed a small proportion of the budget of working-class families (under 9% in 1928–9). From the mid-1920s, the resumption of migration to the cities put intense pressure on the housing stock. In 1926 the official allocation of living space per adult was only 4.9 square metres for workers, 6.9 for employees, and 6.1 for others. Anyone having in excess of that was likely to be asked to 'self-compress' (*samouplotnit'sia*), i.e. to make room for others. With the onset of the First Five-Year Plan the regime returned to a policy of allocating housing on class principles.

With NEP, the attempt to distribute goods and services through the state was abandoned. The easing of supplies that resulted was widely welcomed, but the fact that many goods were beyond the pockets of ordinary folk caused much resentment. From 1926 restrictions on 'speculation' were stepped up, but the state's inability to substitute for private trade led to the emergence of the queue as a characteristic feature of Soviet life. Goods were in eternally short supply – *defitsitnyi*, meaning 'in deficit', was one of many new words that entered the Soviet lexicon – but members of the nomenklatura had access to special shops. Citizens became versed in the arts of getting hold of scarce commodities and services via the back door, cultivating large networks of 'connections'. According to a rhyming jingle by V. V. Mayakovsky, the citizen was ideally set up who had: 'a fiancée in a trust, a godparent in GUM, and a brother in a commissariat' (*nevesta v treste, kum v GUM, brat v narkomat*), GUM being Moscow's leading department store.

Family and gender relations

The Bolsheviks came to power with a radical programme for the liberation of women and transformation of the family. Their reforming zeal was evidenced in the comprehensive Code on Marriage, the Family, and Guardianship, ratified in October 1918, which equalized women's legal status with men's, allowed both spouses to retain the right to their own property and earnings, granted children born outside wedlock the same rights as those born within, and made divorce available upon request. In Bolshevik theory the key to women's liberation lay in taking women out of the confines of the family and bringing them into the sphere of wage work. There they would gain economic independence and develop class consciousness. For this to happen, however, it was recognized that the state would need to take over the tasks of child care and household labour, described by Lenin as 'the most unproductive, the most savage, and the most arduous work a woman can do'. During the first years, women were summoned to set aside their responsibilities to husbands and children and to become fighters on behalf of oppressed humanity. Efrosiniia Marakulina, a peasant who became an instructor in Viatka province, was an archetypal 'new woman': 'She forgot her family, her children, the household. With enthusiasm she threw herself into the new business of enlightening her dark, downtrodden sisters.' Not surprisingly, those who became 'new women' were few. For most women the chaos of the civil war saw them struggling to survive, their lack of interest in the revolutionary drama reinforcing the stereotypical image of the woman as *baba* – 'dark', 'backward', and in thrall to husband and priest.

It was to combat such 'backwardness' that a Women's Bureau was established in 1919 by Inessa Armand and Alexandra Kollontai. They insisted that working women must be mobilized around projects of direct concern to them, such as literacy classes, crèches, collective dining rooms, and consumer cooperatives. During the 1920s the Bureau, which was permanently under-funded, undertook a range of campaigns against wage and hiring discrimination, sexual harassment, layoffs of women, alcoholism, and wife-battering. The assertive feminism that it occasionally encouraged made many men in the party leadership edgy. On 1 March 1927, for example, a conference of working women in Irkutsk passed a resolution declaring that 'it is necessary to fight for the liberation of women and to struggle against men.' In 1927 the Bureau launched an aggressive campaign in Central Asia against the veil, bride price, polygamy, and female segregation. Some 800 women were killed by outraged menfolk, protesting that Bolsheviks were 'turning women into harlots'. This was the excuse that some in the leadership had been looking for. The Bureau was accused of 'heavy-handed bungling', the prelude to its dissolution in 1930.

The Bolsheviks challenged the patriarchal concept that men had a God-given right to rule over women, what Lenin called 'rooting out the "old master right of the man"' but they generally showed far less interest in challenging male than female gender roles. The revolution reconfigured rather than unseated the dominant masculine norm, substituting for the patriarchal model of masculinity a fraternal model in which young men were defined through comradeship and a commitment to the struggle. Within the revolutionary script production took priority over reproduction, so left little space for women whose identities were largely defined by family and motherhood. In pictorial representations of revolution, moreover, women were largely absent. Totemic workers, peasants, and Red Army soldiers were generally men, covertly bolstering the assumption that revolution was men's business. In the course of the 1920s, patriarchal norms quickly gained ascendancy within the party-state, so that gender was one of the first areas in which a 'return of the repressed' became visible.

Many Bolsheviks believed that the family, as an institution based on private property, would be abolished under communism, with the state taking responsibility for the care of children and for domestic labour. In the event, under the blows of war, flight, hunger, and disease, the family began to abolish itself as spouses separated, children were cast adrift, and casual sexual relationships flourished. As a result, the economic position of many women, left to support families without the assistance of menfolk, deteriorated. For poor and vulnerable women, the stability provided by the family came to seem positively desirable and this was one factor behind the rise in the marriage rate during the 1920s: by 1926 the rate was over a third higher than in 1913. With NEP, cuts in state subsidy led to the closure of the public dining halls, crèches, and communal laundries that had been a feature of War Communism, leaving women once again responsible for looking after children, cooking, cleaning, and sewing. These trends, together with the rise in female unemployment, shaped responses to the public debate on the new Family Code of 1926. This simplified divorce procedure, but introduced stricter rules on alimony, making men rather than the state responsible for the upkeep of children. It signalled a shift in thinking towards a view that the family would have to serve as the basic institution of social welfare for a very long time. This chimed with a rising sense that the mounting problems of illegitimacy, abandoned children, hooliganism, and juvenile crime were linked to the breakdown of the family.

If the 1920s saw a strengthening of a more conservative attitude towards the family and marriage, one should not infer that the revolution had had little impact in this area. Within less than a decade, European Russia had the highest divorce rate in the world, divorce being widespread even in rural communities. Similarly, if there was a boom in the birth rate from its nadir of 1922, the long-term trend was towards a decline in the birth rate, especially in the towns, as levels of female education and employment rose and as marriage was delayed. In 1920 Russia became the first country to legalize abortion, a measure motivated by concern that in the prevailing conditions society could not support children properly, rather than by recognition of a woman's right to choose. By the late 1920s, the number of abortions in cities surpassed the number of births, and the typical woman having a termination was married with at least one child.

In the maelstrom of civil war sexual taboos were swept aside. A few in the party saw 'sexual revolution' as intrinsic to the wider social revolution. Kollontai, first Commissar of Social Welfare, demanded 'freedom for winged Eros', by which she meant that women should have the right to autonomy and fulfilment in personal relations. She was widely assumed, however, to be advocating sexual promiscuity. The mainstream of the party looked askance on such thinking, Lenin, in particular, deploring 'hypertrophy in sexual matters'. From the early 1920s exhortations to sublimate sexual energy into constructive activity came thick and fast. The 'psychoneurologist' A. B. Zalkind averred that the 'proletariat at the stage of socialist accumulation is a thrifty, niggardly class and it is not in its interests to allow creative energy to seep into sexual channels'. Such thinking, coloured by contemporary interest in eugenics, put sexuality at the heart of a strategy of social engineering designed to enhance the reproductive and productive capacity of the new society. By the late 1920s, the shift away from permissive attitudes was marked: by 1929 'hardened' prostitutes, once seen as social victims, were being sent to labour camps for wilfully refusing to play their role in production. This increasing emphasis on the danger of sexual anarchy reflected Bolshevik fear that their orderly project risked being engulfed by the libidinal energies of the body and the elemental forces of nature.

Youth: a wavering vanguard

In 1926 the under-twenties made up just over half the rural population. The Bolsheviks looked on children as bearers of the socialist future and concentrated scarce resources on their welfare and education. The notion of childhood as a time of innocence had taken root in late-imperial Russia, and the Bolsheviks built upon the optimism implicit in this idealization. The drastic fall in infant mortality – the scourge of *ancien régime* Russia – and the decline in family size, served to intensify the emotional investment of parents in their child. The Women's Bureau campaigned to improve childcare and discourage practices such as corporal punishment. New limitations on child labour, combined with the lengthening of schooling, delayed entry into adulthood. The Bolsheviks believed that children belonged first and foremost to society, but there was no consensus as to where the line should be drawn between parental and state responsibilities. Not all shared

A. Goikhbarg's view that the state would 'provide vastly better results than the private, individual, unscientific, and irrational approach of individually "loving" but ignorant parents'. Since the state did not have resources to take on the upbringing of children, parents continued to shoulder most of the responsibility, but their right to do so was conditional on performing their duties in accordance with the values of the revolution. 'If fathers persistently try to turn their children into narrow little property owners or mystics, then . . . children have the ethical right to forsake them.'

One of the most horrendous problems facing the Bolsheviks was to deal with the mind-boggling number of orphaned and abandoned children who survived by begging, peddling, or stealing on city streets and in railway stations. The problem had emerged before the First World War, but escalated massively after 1914. By 1922, at least 7 million children, over three-quarters of them boys, had been abandoned. They formed a distinct subculture with their gangs, hierarchies, turf, codes, rituals, and slang. They were a major cause of the sharp rise in juvenile crime. The authorities looked sympathetically on young criminals as social victims, court trials and custodial sentences for juveniles under 17 having been abolished in January 1918. Heroic efforts were made to settle abandoned children in homes and colonies, some of which were run as experimental labour communes based on 'self-government', and by the late 1920s, the number had fallen to around 200,000. By this stage, the failure of juvenile crime to disappear was causing the authorities to take a much less indulgent stance, leading jurists denouncing the 'putrid view that children should not be punished'.

By 1925 the Komsomol had 1.5 million members, which represented a mere 6% of eligible youngsters. From being an exclusively urban organization during the civil war, it struggled to build a rural base and by 1926, 60% of its members were peasants. In the countryside the Komsomol was very much associated with the clash between the generations, young men, and to a lesser extent young women, asserting themselves against their parents over such matters as church attendance. Parents bemoaned the conduct of their offspring: 'Kol'ka has stuck up a picture of Lenin in place of the icon and now goes to rallies, carrying banners and singing scurrilous songs.' In the towns, however, there is evidence that many Komsomol members disliked the ethos of NEP. During the civil war its members had exemplified the heroism, sacrifice, and combativity that were the hallmarks of the time. Now the requisite qualities were 'smartness, discipline, training, and self-organization' and some youngsters appear to have had difficulty knuckling down to the prosaic tasks of economic and cultural construction. The tone of the Komsomol was very much set by young men, since their higher level of literacy, service in the army, experience of seasonal work, and their relative freedom from family obligations gave them a broader view of the world than that of most young women. The proportion of women in the Komsomol nevertheless rose to around one-fifth by the mid-1920s – higher than in the party – but many young women were alienated by the endless routine of meetings, speeches, political education, and demonstrations, and turnover was high.

During NEP young people faced many difficulties, including unemployment, homelessness, and the payment of tuition fees. Official rhetoric cast youth in the role of revolutionary vanguard, but there was much anxiety expressed about the apparent loss of fervour among young people. In 1923 the student newspaper at Petrograd University claimed that only 10% of students actively supported the revolution; that 60% were 'non-party'; that 15% to 20% were 'clearly anti-Soviet'; and that 10% were totally apathetic. The perceived rise in 'hooliganism' seemed to signal a deep social malaise. The young women with red lipstick, bobbed hair, and high heels, and the young men with double-breasted jackets and Oxford bags fed fears that bourgeois decadance was on the increase. The 'epidemic' of suicides that followed that of the poet S. Esenin in December 1925 suggested that many young people had fallen prey to morbid individualism. Finally and paradoxically, the youngsters who turned to religious sects, such as Baptists, Adventists, and Evangelicals, out of attraction to their message of chastity, temperance, restraint, and hard work, often seemed to display a more serious orientation on the world – however sinful they viewed it – than many in the Komsomol. The vagaries of youth, in other words, seemed to strengthen the association of NEP with class aliens, bourgeois restoration, and moral degeneracy.

Cultural revolution

As children of the Enlightenment, the Bolsheviks believed that the dissemination of knowledge and rationality would liberate people from superstition and enhance their freedom and autonomy. Following their intelligentsia forebears, they sought to raise the level of 'culturedness' of a society perceived to be steeped in 'Asiatic' backwardness. 'Culturedness', for the Bolsheviks, could signify anything from punctuality, to clean fingernails, to having a basic knowledge of biology, to carrying out one's trade-union duties efficiently. The promiscuous connotations of its antithesis, 'lack of culture', were neatly captured in a notice pinned on the wharf in Samara: 'Do not throw rubbish about, do not strike a match near the oil pumps, do not spit sunflower seeds, and do not swear or use bad language.' In 1921, following victory on the military and political fronts, 'culture' was declared to be a 'third front' of revolutionary activity. In his last writings Lenin invoked the concept of 'cultural revolution' as vital to the transition to socialism, although his construal of what this revolution entailed proved to be rather modest, centring on the propagation of literacy and solid work habits among the people and the application of science and technology to social development.

The drive to increase literacy was something into which the Bolsheviks put much energy and imagination, aware that active participation in socialist society depended on being able to read. The danger of illiteracy was illustrated in a widely circulated poster that depicted a blindfolded peasant in bast shoes approaching the edge of a cliff with hands outstretched. During the civil war massive effort was focused on the soldiers of the Red Army, but, with NEP, funding for the 'liquidation of literacy' drive was drastically cut back. Even so, by the time of the 1926 census, 51% of the population was literate, compared with 23% in 1897. This was an impressive result, yet it concealed startling disparities. Two-thirds of men in the Soviet Union could read, but only 37% of women. In Turkmenistan 97% of the population was illiterate. Obviously, the educational level of those who went through crash literacy programmes was not high. When 64 soldiers were asked in 1923 to read an article in *Pravda* about the assassination of a Soviet ambassador, none could explain the title: 'The Impertinence of Killers'. Yet learning to read awoke a touching thirst for knowledge. 'Send me a list of books published on comets, stars, water, the earth, and sky.' And as the Bolsheviks well understood, becoming literate also stimulated a desire to learn the language of the new regime, to 'speak Bolshevik'. The efforts of peasants to master the categories that defined the new society were often comical.

> We youth awakening from eternal hibernation and apathy, forming influence in our blood, brightly reflecting the good progresses and initiatives, step by step however slowly (are) moving away from old and rotten throw-backs.

The strange words and locutions of Bolshevik language had an almost magical power.

Other Bolsheviks entertained a more grandiose conception of cultural revolution than Lenin. Bukharin asserted that cultural revolution meant nothing less than a 'revolution in human characteristics, in habits, feelings, and desires, in way-of-life and culture'. From this perspective, its aim was nothing less than the creation of a 'new soviet person' through the total transformation of daily life. In the mid-1920s lively debates took place about the revolutionizing of daily life, which centred on the fraught issue of the relationship of the personal to the political.

At a time when market forces were in the ascendant, when official policies seemed to benefit 'class enemies', progress to socialism seemed peculiarly to depend on the behaviour of individuals. As Krupskaia told the Komsomol congress in 1924: 'Earlier it was perhaps not clear to us that the separation of private life and public life sooner or later leads to the betrayal of communism.' In this context, aspects of daily life as various as dress, hygiene, personal morality, leisure, and the correct use of Russian took on political significance. Was it acceptable for a communist to wear makeup or fashionable clothes? The answer was clearly no, since these things implied an individualistic concern with looking good. Yet the Bolsheviks never eschewed 'bourgeois' values in their entirety. The cultured Soviet citizen was expected to be punctual, efficient, orderly, and neat in appearance; too keen an interest in good manners, nice clothes, or tidy hair, however, could lay one open to the charge of being petty-bourgeois or 'philistine'.

The project to bring about cultural revolution provoked strongest resistance in relation to the major rites of passage – birth, marriage, and death. For centuries these had been marked by religious rituals that had deep existential and cultural resonance. The Bolsheviks grappled to find secular substitutes. The dedication of newborn children, known as Octobering, appears to have been the most successful, albeit only among a small minority. A meeting of the Kremenchug woodturners' union organized a 'red baptism' in January 1924 of girl called 'Ninel' ('Lenin' spelt backwards) in a ceremony that began with an exaltation of 'conscience' and 'reason' against the 'absurd religious rituals which befog and oppress the working class'. Even among communists and Komsomolites, however, such rituals were not popular and many were expelled for having their children baptized or for getting married in church. In particular, the attempt to promote cremation as the rational, economical way of death met almost universal resistance. As late as the 1950s, fewer than half of funerals were secular. People missed the mystery, joy, and ebullience of traditional rituals and found the ersatz substitutes lacking in inward drama and a sense of transcendence.

As an ambitious attempt at social engineering, 'cultural revolution' had a certain coercive element, yet one should be wary of glib generalization about the 'totalitarian' nature of the project, since this overlooks the fact that millions of young people wanted passionately to transform themselves. With the traditional way-of-life so obviously superannuated, many young peasants yearned to become 'cultured': 'Dressed in a cultured fashion I went to the cinema. I really wanted to visit the Park of Culture and Rest but I didn't have enough money.' By 1928 over 12% of letters sent to the *Peasant Newspaper* concerned the 'backwardness' of peasant life. Characteristically they began: 'I am a dark peasant'; 'I write to you from a god-forsaken place'; 'Lying on a dark stove, I am thinking'. Such peasants were gripped by the desire to 'acquire political development and to understand the world', 'to have literature and leadership', lest they become surplus to requirements in the new order. And even the millions who did not warm to the soviet project nevertheless internalized its categories of 'cultured' and 'backward', 'revolutionary' and 'reactionary'.

The attack on religion

The early 1920s generally saw the regime relax its policies, but from 1922 to the death of Patriarch Tikhon in 1925 it launched a sustained assault on the Orthodox Church. In February 1922 the Bolsheviks ordered the Church to surrender its valuables to aid the victims of the famine. This provoked a sharp clash in Shuia, in which four were killed and ten injured. In private Lenin discarded the pretence that the seizures were intended to assist famine victims – 'we shall secure for ourselves a fund of several hundred million rubles' – and ordered that the Shuia 'insurrectionists' be tried. Eight priests, two men, and one woman were duly executed and 25 imprisoned. In Petrograd, where popular agitation against the seizures had an anti-semitic character, Metropolitan Veniamin and three others were tried and executed. It has been claimed that there were 1,414 clashes with believers in 1922–3 in which over 7,000 priests, monks, and nuns disappeared, most apparently killed.

In May 1922 the Orthodox Church succumbed to a damaging schism. A group of radical priests, known as Renovationists, came out in support of soviet power and forced the abdication of the 'counter-revolutionary' Tikhon. They called a church council in 1923, which passed a series of reforms long under discussion that included the replacement of Church Slavonic with vernacular Russian, the adoption of the Gregorian calendar, and greater participation by the laity in services and diocesan administration. By 1925, two-thirds of parishes had formally affiliated to the Renovationists. Yet these 'rationalizing' reforms were not popular with a laity whose faith was intimately bound up with the observance of feast days and the cult of local saints and shrines. Moreover, the laity were in a position to impede their implementation since the revolution had strengthened their control of parish affairs; and the clergy, who were the chief supporters of the reforms, relied on them for financial support. In June 1923 the Bolsheviks withdrew support from the Renovationists after Tikhon expressed loyalty to the regime. Many of the faithful questioned his act of accommodation, yet were nevertheless delighted as Tikhon set out to destroy the Renovationists. In the immediate term, this merely deepened the schism, but by the late 1920s the Renovationists were routed. By the time his successor, Metropolitan Sergei, pledged loyalty to the soviets in May 1927, it was clear that the church was one organization that the regime was going to have to live with.

The policy adopted towards sectarians and Old Believers – those who broke away from the Orthodox Church in the second half of the 17th century after Patriarch Nikon (1605–81) introduced liturgical reforms – was more conciliatory, since the regime viewed them as politically more progressive, in view of the persecution which they had suffered under tsarism, their emphasis on hard work, sobriety, and strict moral standards, and their openness to forming agricultural communes. Old Believers and sectarians were thus allowed to publish journals, organize conferences, charities, and cooperatives. Even in the early 1920s, however, the OGPU kept a strict eye on them, pursuing a tactic of divide and rule. After 1926, as policy towards the Orthodox Church eased somewhat, policy towards the sects – as well as to Islam and Judaism – toughened. Only in 1929, however, with the onset of Stalin's 'revolution from above', did the regime unleash a full-scale onslaught on all forms of organized religion.

Despite its confrontation with Orthodoxy, the government viewed the battle against religion as a long-term matter of education and propaganda. In 1922 Emelian Iaroslavsky founded a weekly newspaper to propagate atheism among the masses which, incidentally, counted the years from 1917. In 1925 he founded the League of Militant Godless to oppose the anti-religious zealots in the Komsomol, known as 'priest-eaters', who revelled in offending believers by such antics as burning icons and turning pigs loose in church. By contrast, the League favoured public debate with believers on topics such as whether the world was created in six days. Clergy inveighed against the godless as 'debauchers and libertines' and villagers, who now paid for the upkeep of schools, ensured that atheistic propaganda was kept out of the classroom. By 1930 the League claimed to have more than 2 million members; but its record of achievement was unimpressive. Religious observance was on the decline, especially in the cities, but this had more to do with the urbanization, army service, the culture of the radio and newspaper, and the increase in technology than with atheistic propaganda as such. In some ways the history of religion under NEP was less about the clash between church and state than about the clash between a modernizing culture, backed by the resources of the state, and the local communities whose identity was closely bound up with religion.

Despite its militant atheism, the Stalin faction did not scruple to buttress its legitimacy by sanctifying the dead Lenin, inscribing elements of popular religion into the official political culture. During his lifetime Lenin had been adulated but was never strictly the object of a cult. His death, however, aroused popular anxiety expressed in rumours of foreign invasion, economic collapse, and a split in the party. The

We residents of the Il'ich settlement, being workers at the Hammer and Sickle, the Kursk railway workshops, the Russian Cable, and other nearby factories, turn to the Soviet with a practical request. Our settlement is sited on land formerly belonging to the Vsekhsviatskii monastery, which passed to us as one of the gains of the October Revolution. But that gain has not been realized to the full. Having turned this lair of spongers into a workers' settlement we wish, in addition, to erect on the site of the church, that fortress of reaction, a model workers' community, a fortress to the new way-of-life, with comfortable housing, leisure facilities, and rational recreations. But difficulties arise from the slowness of certain soviet organs and from lack of finance. We thus request the Moscow Soviet to issue an instruction to allow for the speedy sale of church property.

Declaration of 153 workers of the Il'ich settlement to the Moscow Soviet, March 1924

Stalin group responded by sedulously cultivating the myth of Lenin as the incarnation of the proletariat – 'Lenin is with us always and everywhere' – tapping into a deep-seated need for a father figure who would take care of his people. In every club, school, and factory, the Lenin corner replaced the icon corner. Bolsheviks, who hitherto had fought to expose the popular belief that saints' bodies did not decompose, now embalmed Lenin's body like that of some latter-day pharaoh, and placed it in a sacred shrine. It is hard to say how far the regime used the Lenin cult to impose its values on the populace and how far it was responding to popular needs.

The intelligentsia and the arts

The October Revolution gave birth to an astonishing burst of artistic experiment that was unsurpassed anywhere else in the world. It was

18. The model of Vladimir Tatlin's *Monument to the Third International*

symbolized in K. S. Malevich's *Black Square*, V. Y. Tatlin's *Monument to the Third International*, V. Y. Meyerhold's biomechanical drama, the transrational poetry of V. Khlebnikov, the strident verses of V. V. Mayakovsky, and N. Roslavets's experiments with a new tonal system in music. The avant-garde, which had emerged around 1908, was impelled by the belief that the revolutionization of artistic practice was part of a larger project of transforming the role of art within society, art having the power to transform 'life'. Though divided over aesthetic matters, the avant-garde was loosely leftist in politics and iconoclastic in spirit, though by no means all endorsed the Futurist call to 'Throw Pushkin, Dostoevsky, Tolstoy overboard from the ship of modernity.' Many of its representatives, such as Malevich, A. M. Rodchenko, Tatlin, and Kandinsky in the visual arts, gained positions of influence within new soviet institutions.

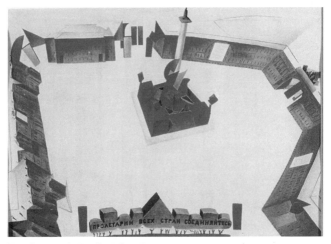

19. Altman's design for Palace Square

Theatre was supreme among the arts during the civil war. However, Meyerhold's efforts to unleash a 'Theatrical October' were blocked by the Commissar of Enlightenment, Lunacharsky, who insisted on the importance of preserving the classical repertoire. Lunacharsky defended the principle of artistic pluralism but supported the avant-garde, whereas Lenin was far less tolerant, condemning it as 'absurd and perverted'. With the onset of NEP, architecture, film and the novel came into their own. Constructivism was the one movement in the visual arts born directly out of October 1917. In seeking to fuse the artistic and technological aspects of production, it aspired to create an environment in which the 'new soviet person' could flourish. Constructivist interest in the properties of materials and in industrial design had a huge impact on modern architecture, on photography, print graphics, fabrics, furniture, and film. In cinema leading directors such as S. Eisenstein, D. Vertov, V. Pudovkin, and A. Dovzhenko, some of whom had cut their teeth making propaganda 'shorts' during the civil war, produced classics of world cinema. Most experimented with montage – the juxtaposition of unexpected images – as a way of expanding the visual awareness of the audience. As in all other artistic fields, there was vigorous debate – over the virtues of documentary as opposed to feature film, of propaganda as opposed to entertainment. However, even Eisenstein's politically impeccable films had a lukewarm reception from officialdom, not to speak of the public, because of their experimental editing, shooting, and mise-en-scène. The revival of commercial mass culture that came about with NEP, moreover, left no doubt that the public preferred escapist fiction, light music, comedy, and variety acts to avant-garde art. Official concern that art should become more accessible was one reason why in the second half of the 1920s the regime came to look with increasing favour on those artists who had continued to work within broadly realist and figurative genres.

Literature experienced an efflorescence in the 1920s, partly because of the revival of private publishing houses. Some of the first responses to revolution, from poets such as A. A. Blok, S. A. Esenin and A. Belyi, had had an apocalyptic character, identifying with its 'spiritual maximalism'. B. Pil'niak's *Naked Year* (1922), considered by many to be the first 'soviet' novel, depicted the revolution as a vengeful, Asiatic force stripping off the civilized veneer of 'mechanical Europe'. K. Fedin, M. Zoshchenko, and V. Ivanov, by contrast, hailed the revolution as a liberation of the fantastic imagination. They came under attack for being 'ideologically empty' from the Smithy group, which lauded collectivism, labour, and the cult of the machine. As the memory of the civil war faded, writing began to become less partisan and more reflective of the uncertainties of NEP. Noteworthy was the tragicomic satire of M. Zoshchenko, whose subject-matter was the absurdity of daily life. A humanistic, apolitical aesthetic also gained ground in the poetry of Mandelstam and Akhmatova, who aspired to cultivate lyricism and a language of precision, clarity, and restraint. It was in reaction to such pluralism that in 1928 the Association of Proletarian Writers demanded that literature obey a 'social command'. This aesthetic, which saw fiction as having little value except as sociological document, chimed with the tastes of newly literate readers who craved positive, unambiguous characters, a

20. Constructivist poster design for Dziga Vertov's film, *The Eleventh*

secure narrative, and moral certainties. Yet if the 1920s saw genuine pluralism in literature, it also saw the steady rise of censorship. In 1922 the Main Directorate for the Protection of State Secrets in the Press was set up, charged with censoring domestic and imported printed works, manuscripts, and photos. By July 1924, 216 foreign films had been banned because of the 'threat to the ideological education of workers and peasants in our country'. This was stricter censorship than had pertained after 1905.

During the 1920s the position of the intelligentsia remained ambivalent. Having reduced it to political impotence, the regime encouraged it to put its expertise to the service of socialism since it needed teachers, scientists, planners, managers, doctors, and engineers. From the mid-1920s, salaries began to rise and material privileges to accrue. The regime, however, continued to distrust the intelligentsia as a competing elite with pretensions to moral leadership, one likely to impede its efforts to establish hegemony. Whilst a degree of pluralism was tolerated in education, the arts, and the sciences, the trend was clearly towards increased official control. In 1922 universities lost their autonomy – in spite of a strike by academics in Moscow and elsewhere – and the State Academic Council began rather tentatively to weed out 'theologians, mystics, and representatives of extreme idealism'. Uniquely, the Academy of Sciences preserved its autonomy until 1929, although a Red Academy was created to compete with it. Associations as seemingly innocuous as the Vegetarian Society were regularly refused authorization by OGPU 'for political considerations'. Nevertheless the extraordinary fact is that in spite of all its travails, the intelligentsia maintained a distinct social identity through its informal networks, personal ties and institutional loyalties.

The 1920s was thus an era of unbounded artistic and intellectual diversity yet one that saw the regime steadily intensify its control of cultural life through censorship, control of funding, and brusque intervention. Since it believed in the power of art to transform human consciousness, it was not going to allow its direction to be determined by the spontaneous whims of the individual artist or by the imperatives of the marketplace. Moreover, the gap between the avant-garde and popular taste troubled a leadership that recognized the tremendous propaganda potential of such new media as film. Stalin, an aficionado of the cinema, described it as 'the most important means of mass agitation'. Finally, the tendency of the party to take a less tolerant attitude to the avant-garde was an indirect reflection of the party's own increasing concern with stability and its repudiation of anything that smacked of permanent revolution. That said, the exercise of party control was never secure or efficient in this period and debate about what constituted an appropriate art for a socialist society remained relatively free. A qualitative difference exists between the diversity of the 1920s – however compromised – and the stifling conformism of the 1930s.

By highlighting the disparity between ideal and reality, NEP may be seen as reining in the utopianism of the civil war, but one should not conclude that utopianism died. The hopes placed in electrification, Taylorism, and cultural revolution were utopian and evinced the ongoing dynamism of the regime. However, Russian realities were beginning to make themselves felt. Paradoxically, as the regime stabilized so the deeper structuring forces of Russian development reasserted themselves: forces of geography (huge distances, scattered populations, inadequate communications), climate (the risk attached to agriculture), geopolitics (the difficulty of defending frontiers), the underdevelopment of the market and the paucity of capital, the deeply ingrained patterns of peasant culture, the traditions of the bureaucratic state. The Bolsheviks, who had so categorically rejected Russia's heritage, found that the greater the distance they travelled from October, the more these forces made themselves felt. This did not mean that they became captive to those forces, nor that impulses to revolutionary transformation exhausted themselves: Stalin's 'revolution from above' was to prove the contrary. But in many areas one can see a distancing from early iconoclasm and the beginning of a synthesis of revolution and tradition.

Conclusion

In the most trenchant recent interpretation of Soviet history, Martin Malia has argued that the Soviet Union was an 'ideocracy' whose development was driven by the Bolshevik desire to realize a millenarian vision of communism through the abolition of private property, profit, the market, and civil society. Many agree with Malia that ideology constitutes the key to understanding the development of Soviet totalitarianism, but there is little agreement as to which particular elements in Marxism-Leninism are to blame. Some *endorse Malia's view that* the seeds of totalitarianism *lay* in Marx's aspiration to abolish private property; others point to his belief in class struggle as the motor of history or to his assertion that the proletariat must exercise a dictatorship during the transition to socialism. Others point to more general features of Marxism such as its claim to provide 'scientific' knowledge of the laws of history or its rejection of morality as a constraint on action. No doubt some, and possibly all, of these elements in Marxism played a part in shaping the course of Soviet history. The fact that there is uncertainty as to which particular elements were decisive, however, should make us pause before underwriting a view that in ideology lies the root of all evil. This is especially so when we consider that in 1917 the elements of Marxism that appealed were very different from those mentioned above: the promise to end inequality and exploitation, and the promise to abolish the state and vest power in the hands of the toiling people.

It is beyond question that ideology was of central importance in determining the course of the Bolshevik revolution. All Bolsheviks – including Stalin – believed in the Marxist vision and it is impossible to comprehend the scale of their ambition, their astounding energy, and their ruthless determination unless one takes the ideas that inspired them seriously. Their victory in the civil war, for example, is inexplicable except in terms of their unwavering conviction that they were exercising dictatorship on behalf of a temporarily 'declassed' proletariat. However, the civil war also reminds us that Bolshevik ideology *changed* over time, in many respects profoundly. In 1917 Lenin spent valuable time developing Marx's notion of the withering away of the state. By 1918 Lenin's *State and Revolution* was an irrelevance. Within months, Lenin had come to see in the massive strengthening of the state the sole guarantee of advance towards socialism. Not all Bolsheviks agreed. Through the civil war and into the 1920s, Bolsheviks understood their ideology in different ways – the barracks' vision of communist society associated with War Communism, the productivist vision associated with NEP – and the sharp disagreements that arose out of these differing perspectives were just as important in determining the course of the revolution as the beliefs and values shared in common. By

21. Demonstration: 'Let us direct our path towards the shining life.'

presenting Bolshevism as monolithic and unchanging, the 'ideocracy' thesis radically simplifies the ways in which ideas – and conflict over ideas – shaped the conduct of the Bolsheviks.

If we look back on the developments described in this book, all too often it is the Bolsheviks' incapacity to realize their ends, their blindness rather than their vision, that is striking. After they came to power, they faced a huge array of problems for which Marxism-Leninism left them ill-equipped. Ideology could not tell them, for instance, whether or not to sign the Treaty of Brest-Litovsk. Policy, therefore, was frequently the outcome of improvisation and pragmatism as much of the hallowed tenets of ideology. In other words, the relationship between belief and action was complex, influenced by a far larger range of factors than the 'ideocracy' thesis allows. If ideology was critical in shaping the institutions and practices of the Soviet state, so were geography, geopolitics, economic and political structures, the specific conjunctures thrown up by revolution, civil war, and a shattered economy and, not least, events that no one foresaw. All of these things were interpreted through the lens of ideology, so their significance is inseparable from the meanings with which they were invested. Nevertheless they exercised a weight of determination in their own right and cannot be reduced to ideology. Throughout the period we have looked at, the 'real world' – whether in the shape of a railway system brought to paralysis, the ravages of typhus, or a dazzling military offensive by Denikin – had a nasty habit of sneaking up on the Bolsheviks from behind, throwing into confusion their best-laid plans.

The story we have traced has been in part one about how possibilities opened up in 1917 were steadily closed off. As early as January 1918, key components of the 1917 revolution – power to the soviets, workers' control of production, the abolition of the standing army – were jettisoned. By 1921 the Bolsheviks no longer saw the working class as the agent of revolution, but the party-state and the Red Army. This narrowing of the meaning of the revolution had less to do with ideology than with the structural logic of the Bolsheviks' situation. In the teeth of determined political opposition and intense popular resistance, they came to rely on force. They had little difficulty justifying this in ideological terms, but the logic that drove them down the path to one-party dictatorship was structural more than it was ideological. Otherwise it is hard to explain why they formed a coalition with the Left SRs or displayed a certain fastidiousness in banning opposition parties outright. The belief that the end justified the means served them well, blinding them to the way in which means corrupt ends. In August 1919 the newspaper *Red Sword* proclaimed: 'Everything is permitted to us because we are the first in the world to raise the sword not in the name of enserfment and oppression but of general happiness and liberation from slavery.' Very quickly, however, liberation from slavery had been fatally subverted by the means chosen to achieve it.

The meaning of the revolution also changed as it became embedded in the Russian environment. By the 1920s, the Bolsheviks were responding to many of the same pressures – the need rapidly to industrialize, to modernize agriculture, to build defence capability – that had motivated Nicholas II's regime. These aims were now articulated very differently, but the objective exigencies of modernization made themselves felt nevertheless. The revolution was redefined as an authoritarian form of modernization in which the state would mobilize the human and material resources of an impoverished country to industrialize, modernize agriculture, and raise the cultural level of the people. This required, in particular, breaking the passive resistance of the peasantry in order to provide capital for what Preobrazhensky called 'primitive socialist accumulation'. Ideology adapted to these deeper structural and cultural constraints as much as it inspired the drive to escape them.

This is to paint a rather bleak picture, since it implies that the vicious circle of economic backwardness and international isolation could not have been broken without the use of coercion by the state. This did not mean, however, that the Bolsheviks were deprived of political agency: they faced real choices at each turning-point. It is ironic that those most inclined to depict the Bolsheviks as conscious architects of tyranny – i.e. who ascribe to them a large degree of agency – attach so little importance to the actual choices they made. Yet logically, if the relationship of agency to circumstances was skewed so heavily in favour of the former, then opting for Bukharin's course or Trotsky's course, instead of Stalin's, should have had a marked impact on future developments. However, such analysts deny that there was much at stake in the inner-party struggle. Even if, as has been argued, Bukharin and Trotsky were engaged in fundamentally the same enterprise as Stalin – socialism as it was understood in 1917 having long ceased to be on the cards – it is still quite reasonable to insist that if either had defeated Stalin, the horror and bloodshed of the 1930s could have been avoided.

This raises the central question of the relationship of Leninism to Stalinism. Were the horrors of Stalinism inscribed in the logic of Leninism? No less a person than the young Trotsky warned in 1904 of the logic of Lenin's views on party organization:

> The party apparatus at first substitutes itself for the party as a whole; then the Central Committee substitutes itself for the apparatus; and finally a single 'dictator' substitutes himself for the Central Committee.

Yet in later life Trotsky vehemently denied that there were continuities between Leninism and Stalinism, insisting that a whole 'river of blood' separated the two. It is beyond question that there was much in Leninist theory and practice that adumbrated Stalinism. Lenin was architect of the party's absolute monopoly on power; it was he who ruthlessly subordinated the soviets and trade unions. It was he who refused to give any quarter to those who thought differently, who eliminated a free press, who crushed the socialist opposition, who banned the right of party members to form factions. He even went so far as to suggest that the will of the proletariat 'may sometimes be carried out by a dictator'. Lenin, in other words, must bear considerable responsibility for the institutions, the climate of intolerance, and the legal and moral nihilism that allowed Stalin to come to power. But this argument has suggested that while there was a logic at work, it was not the inexorable logic of an unfolding idea, but one inscribed in the interaction of certain ideological goals and organizational principles with structural and circumstantial pressures.

If many of the features typical of Stalinism can be traced back to before 1928, the so-called 'Great Break', instituted by the First Five-Year Plan and forced collectivization, was exactly that – a break in policy that unleashed devastating and wrenching change upon society. Living under Stalin was a very different experience from living under NEP, and to deny any element of discontinuity is to fail imaginatively to appreciate the murderous nature of Stalinism. The institutions of rule may not have changed, but personal dictatorship, the unrestrained use of force, the cult of power, endemic fear, a stifling conformism, paranoia about encirclement and internal wreckers, the unleashing of terror used against a whole society, all meant that political life was qualitatively different from under Lenin. Of course, terror, forced labour, and show trials had their antecedents under Lenin, but quantity had become transformed into quality. In accelerating the economic modernization of the Soviet Union, Stalin believed he was continuing the revolution. Yet he stamped out any residual emancipatory impulses, presiding over the consolidation of a leviathan state in which a ruling elite enjoyed power and privilege at the expense of the mass of the people, and in which forms of patriarchy and Russian chauvinism were reconstituted.

A related question concerns the extent to which Stalinism represented the resurgence of deeply rooted elements in Russia's political culture. The cultural continuity argument is central to Richard Pipes's influential account of the Russian Revolution. It rests on the idea that tsarism was a patrimonial regime in which the tsar's absolute and unconstrained authority derived from his ownership of the country's resources, including the lives of his subjects. Under tsarism the peasantry, Pipes avers, were politically passive, accepting of autocracy, and lacking a sense of civic responsibility. The preceding account has emphasized that the revolution released a flood of change that massively destabilized cultural norms and practices. Yet it has endorsed elements of the cultural continuity argument, pointing to how in the 1920s a 'return of the repressed' was in operation. The similarity between taken-for-granted orientations to politics under tsarism and Stalinism is striking – the primacy of the state vis-à-vis society, the personalized relationship between people and ruler, the lack of legal restraints on power, the absence of institutions mediating between rulers and ruled, clientelism as a way of building social and political relationships, and mistrust towards the outside world. Moshe Lewin has argued that there is a 'contamination effect' of tradition, whereby the quicker customary patterns are broken, the more likely they are to reassert themselves in the longer term. At the same time, and contra Pipes, one must be cautious about interpreting Russia's political culture as a monolithic system. Culture is a contested field of relatively empowered norms and practices. In 1917 democracy – of a very particular kind – flourished, so one has to explain why this gave way to impulses to authoritarianism. Moreover, rather than treat political culture as a causal factor explaining the rise of Stalinism, it is better to view it as a conditioning context, in which norms and practices shape political action negatively by providing few resources to counter the reimposition of authoritarian rule. Finally, Stalinism was never traditional authoritarianism writ large: it synthesized many elements of the Russian national tradition with Leninism, its character as a mobilizing party-state making it very much a creature of the 20th century.

Nor should the 'return of the repressed' be read as signifying that the impact of the revolution was shallow. A theme of the book has been that an antagonistic perception of the social order bit deep into popular culture, that commitment to equality was widespread, and that the ideal of soviet power was hugely popular. What motivated much resistance to the Bolsheviks was precisely the sense that they were betraying those ideals. The revolution, however, always meant different things to different people and different things to the same people at different times. It could mean being forcibly conscripted into the Red Army, unimaginable hardship for cold and hungry townspeople, outsiders coming into one's village and seizing grain, or upstarts from one's own village behaving corruptly as representatives of soviet power. Alternatively, it could mean the chance to learn to read, not losing one's child to disease, increasing the size of one's household plot, getting a divorce from a drunken husband, or being schooled in one's native tongue.

Social identities remained fractured and unsettled, yet they had undergone profound transformation as a result of the revolution. Class had provided the dominant language through which political allegiances were constituted in 1917 and it continued to be dominant in the new order. One is struck by the speed with which peasants took up the language of class – eagerly seeking to prove, for example, that they were not kulaks – although whether this was as a means of self-protection, of legitimating complaints, or of explaining away their problems is anyone's guess. This happened so quickly because the Bolshevik discourse of class was superimposed on an already existing sense of 'them' and 'us'. At the same time, it is clear that peasant perceptions of rural society continued to be at odds with those of the communists. Poor peasants, the cynosure of the party leadership, were often considered 'idlers' and 'spongers' by fellow villagers, whereas kulaks might be praised for their industriousness or castigated as 'commune eaters' and 'parasites on the mir'. Nevertheless, the deployment of class distinctions as the basis of official policy, such as in granting tax exemptions or in encouraging poor peasants to form separate organizations after 1926, did much to focus social identities around them. By extension, the millions of peasants who petitioned the authorities or wrote to the press wrote themselves into the new order in the very act of writing, their little text forming a fragment of the Big Text written by the state. In other words, notwithstanding the widespread resistance to the repression and social engineering of the party-state, Bolshevik ideology provided a basis on which millions in this highly fluid society could fashion an identity, however fragile.

So far as workers were concerned, class in some respects weakened as a social identity, which may help explain why the level of collective protest declined in the 1920s. In its propaganda the party-state constantly hammered away at the notion that the proletariat was the ruling class, and in spite of poor living and working conditions, workers did enjoy certain privileges relative to other social groups. The state had become the powerful exponent of the discourse of class, with power to determine its strategic uses through the mass media, organs of censorship, schools and the like. So the language that had been used by workers since 1905 to articulate grievances lost much of its oppositional force. Workers could still use it – especially to contrast rhetoric with reality – but through use of such categories as 'conscious' and 'backward' workers, through the idea of disaffection as an expression of 'petty-bourgeois' consciousness, the state did much to emasculate a language that in 1917 had served to knit together the disparate elements of the workforce into a self-conscious political force.

The transformation of social identities took place along many other dimensions than that of class. The category of 'woman' acquired a new salience after 1917, but never to the point that it challenged the implicitly masculine construction of the revolutionary script. And for every 'new woman', there were a thousand whose lack of response to the drama of revolution appeared to reinforce a view of the female sex as 'backward'. Similarly, for those in their 20s and younger, 'youth' became a category through which a very empowering identity could be constructed, aligning them with the forces of culture and socialism, legitimizing their rebellion against 'backward' parents. Yet the high-minded construction of youth inherent in official ideology strained

22. Red Square caricatures

against less rigorous, more hedonistic notions of what it meant to be free of the responsibilities of adulthood.

Finally, one may note the paradoxical development of national identity in this period. For non-Russians the 1920s were a period when national identities flourished, leaving Russian identity in something of a limbo. They were also a time when among the more politicized, a distinctively Soviet identity gained ground for the first time. There were genuinely internationalist aspects to this identity, yet it also covertly ascribed superiority to Russian culture and endorsed the political dominance of Slavs. Popular Russian national identity had been growing in the late-imperial period, but had retreated under the onslaught of class in 1917. As early as the civil war, however – which Radek characterized as a 'national struggle of liberation against foreign intervention' – the defence of the Soviet motherland began to refocus latent patriotic sentiment. Similarly, Stalin's doctrine of 'socialism on one country' served as code for sentiment that Russia was not a whit inferior to the capitalist West. In other words, whilst Soviet identity was never simply Russian national identity, as the Soviet Union developed, elements of Russian national identity that had once been taboo were tacitly recuperated.

The Bolshevik revolution wrought calamity on a scale commensurate with the transformation in the human condition that it sought to achieve. Measured by the benchmarks of contemporary politics, Bolshevik ambition leaves us reeling. But it is easier for us today to appreciate the illusions under which they laboured than the ideals they sought to achieve. Yet we shall never understand the Russian Revolution unless we appreciate that the Bolsheviks were fundamentally driven by outrage against the exploitation at the heart of capitalism and the aggressive nationalism that had led Europe into the carnage of the First World War. The hideous inhumanities that resulted from the revolution, culminating in Stalinism, should not obscure the fact that millions welcomed the revolution as the harbinger of social justice and freedom.

At a philosophical level, the revolution raised profound questions about how justice, equality, and freedom can be reconciled that are still relevant today, even if the answers the Bolsheviks gave to those questions were fatally flawed. We live in a world where it has become hard to think critically about the principles on which society is organized. Everything conspires to make us acquiesce in the world as it is, to discourage the belief that it can be radically reordered on more just and equal lines. Yet that is precisely what the Bolsheviks undertook to achieve. I write at a time when there has been a rise in 'anti-capitalist' protests, motivated by revulsion at the staggering inequalities that characterize our world. As the 21st century dawns, it seems safe to conclude that there will be elements in the Russian Revolution that continue to inspire, even as there are many that will stand as a dreadful warning.

Further reading

The following readings are general books that have mainly appeared during the last decade. They will allow the reader to pursue the subject of the Russian Revolution in further detail. No reference is made to the specialist literature, references to which will be found in the bibliographies of the books cited.

Two extremely useful volumes on which this book has drawn extensively are:

Harold Shukman (ed.), *The Blackwell Encyclopedia of the Russian Revolution* (Oxford, 1988) and Edward Acton *et al.* (eds.), *Critical Companion to the Russian Revolution, 1914–1921* (London, 1997).

Russia under the tsars

An excellent survey of Russia under the tsars: Geoffrey Hosking, *Russia: People and Empire, 1552–1917* (London, 1997). A very readable account of Russia during the First World War: W. Bruce Lincoln, *A Passage through Armageddon: the Russians in War and Revolution* (Oxford, 1986).

The revolution

A scintillating account of the revolution: Orlando Figes, *A People's Tragedy: the Russian Revolution, 1891–1924* (London, 1996). Also worth consulting (though an arraignment rather than analysis of the

revolution): Richard Pipes, *The Russian Revolution* (New York, 1990).
Good accounts of 1917: Rex A. Wade, *The Russian Revolution, 1917*
(Cambridge University Press, 2000); James D. White, *The Russian
Revolution, 1917–21* (London, 1994). Sharp on interpretations of the
revolution: Edward Acton, *Rethinking the Russian Revolution* (London,
1990). Two collections of more specialist pieces: E. R. Frankel *et al.*
(eds.), *Revolution in Russia: Reassessments of 1917* (Cambridge, 1992);
Robert Service (ed.), *Society and Politics in the Russian Revolution*
(London, 1992).

The civil war period

Good, reliable accounts of the civil war period: Christopher Read, *From
Tsar to Soviets: the Russian People and their Revolution, 1917–21* (London,
1996); Evan Mawdsley, *The Russian Civil War* (London, 1987); Geoffrey
Swain, *Russia's Civil War* (Stroud, 2000). A collection of uniformly strong
essays from which many of the insights of these chapters are drawn:
Diane P. Koenker, William G. Rosenberg, and Ronald Grigor Suny (eds.),
Party, State, and Society in the Russian Civil War (Bloomington, 1989).

The economy and NEP

Major studies of the economy: Silvana Malle, *The Economic Organization
of War Communism, 1918–1921* (Cambridge University Press, 1985);
R. W. Davies (ed.), *From Tsarism to the New Economic Policy* (London,
1990); R. W. Davies, Mark Harrison, and S. G. Wheatcroft, *The Economic
Transformation of the Soviet Union, 1913–1945* (Cambridge, 1994). On NEP
the following can be warmly recommended: Lewis H. Siegelbaum,
Soviet State and Society between Revolutions, 1918–1929 (Cambridge,
1992); Vladimir Brovkin, *Russia After Lenin: Politics, Culture and Society*
(Routledge, London, 1998); Sheila Fitzpatrick, Alexander Rabinowitch,
Richard Stites (eds.), *Russia in the Era of NEP: Explorations in Soviet Society
and Culture* (Indiana University Press, Bloomington, 1991). Many insights
in chapters 4 and 5 are drawn from: Moshe Lewin, *The Making of the
Soviet System* (London, 1985); V. P. Danilov (trans. and ed. Orlando
Figes), *Rural Russia Under the New Regime* (Hutchinson, London, 1988);

Graeme Gill, *The Origins of the Stalinist Political System* (Cambridge University Press, 1990),

Lenin and Stalin

On Lenin: Beryl Williams, *Lenin* (London, 2000); Robert Service, *Lenin: A Biography* (London, 2000). On Stalin there is the monumental two-volume biography by Robert C. Tucker, *Stalin as Revolutionary: 1879–1929* (New York, 1973) and *Stalin in Power: the Revolution from Above, 1928–1941* (New York, 1990).

Essays and general histories

Important essays are to be found in Sheila Fitzpatrick (ed.), *Stalinism: New Directions* (Routledge, London, 2000). General histories of the Soviet Union that can be recommended: Martin Malia, *The Soviet Tragedy: A History of Socialism in Russia, 1917–1991* (New York, 1994); Ronald G. Suny, *The Soviet Experiment: Russia, the USSR and the Successor States* (New York, 1998); Peter Kenez, *A History of the Soviet Union from the Beginning to the End* (Cambridge, 1999); Robert Service, *A History of Twentieth-Century Russia* (London, 1997).

Index

A

Abkhazia 124
Abortion 140
Academy of Sciences 155
Agriculture 8, 102–3
Akhmatova, A. 153
Alekseev, M. V. 16
Alexandra, Empress 13
All-Russian Communist Party
    (RKP(b) 1918–25; VKP(b)
    1925–52) 66, 69–70
    authoritarianism of 67, 69, 97,
        98; Central Committee of
        66–7, 116; changing culture
        of 67, 98; internal party
        struggle 111–13, 126–7; low
        level of political education
        of 117; membership of 68,
        116; Old Bolsheviks 98, 117;
        Orgburo 67, 115; party
        control commission 117;
        Politburo 67, 115; purges of
        116; Secretariat 67, 115, 116;
        workers in 68, 114, 116–17;
    Congresses of: eighth 49, 68;
        tenth 68, 75, 100;
        fourteenth 111;
    See also Bolshevik party
Allied intervention 48, 54, 55, 61,
    72
Anarchists 24, 30, 34, 64
Anti-semitism 51, 64, 108, 131
Antonov, A. S. 90

Armand, I. 138
Armenia 27, 40, 48, 57, 122
Army, Russian imperial 5, 12,
    15–16, 22, 24–5, 32, 38, 44
    See also First World War,
        Sailors
Association of Proletarian
    Writers 153
Astrakhan 93
Autocracy, crisis of 6, 8–14
Avant-garde art 150–3, 155
Azerbaijan 48, 57, 122, 124

B

Baku 57
'Baggers' 76, 80
Banks, nationalization of 73,
    85
Basmachi (bandits) 60, 61
    See also Muslims
Belorussia 55, 56, 90, 122
Belyi, A. 153
Berdiaev, N. A. 87
Birth rate 140
Bliukher, V. K. 52
Blok, A.A. 153
Bolshevik party 22–4, 25, 34, 35,
    44
    Central Committee of 35, 41–2;
        dictatorship of 62–71, 95–6;
        evolves into party of
        government 67, 96–7; non-
        Russian nationalities and
        55–60, 62, 162; membership
        of 24; Military Opposition
        49; policy towards socialist

opposition 65–6;
utopianism of 40, 156;
See also All-Russian
Communist Party; October
seizure of power
Bourgeoisie, industrial and
commercial 9–10, 15, 30, 31,
85–6
See also Burzhui
Brest-Litovsk, Treaty of 42, 73
Brusilov, A. A. 13
Buchanan, G. W. 14.
Bukhara 26, 61, 122
Bukharin, N. I. 55, 67, 75, 97, 101,
111, 112, 127, 145, 161
Bulgakov, M.A. 135
'Bureaucracy' in party-state 69,
71, 86–7, 97, 98–9, 108, 111,
117–18
Burzhui 32, 80, 85, 95

C

Censorship 154, 155
Central Asia (Turkestan) 26,
60–1, 138–9
Central Industrial Region 10, 29,
45
Chechnya 122
Cheka (GPU 1922–23; OGPU
1923–34) 53, 62–4, 65, 69,
80, 86, 92, 94, 108, 118, 148,
155
Chernov, V.M. 21, 31, 44, 96
Children 138, 139, 141–2
infant mortality 8, 141;
Octobering 146; orphans 142

Chukhovsky, K. 68
Church, Russian Orthodox 11, 42,
54, 87–8, 147–50
See also Clergy
Cinema 152–3, 154, 155
Civil society 9,
Civil war 46–55
Class, discourse of 31–2, 88, 126,
131–2, 164–5
division between 'them' and
'us' 19, 31, 88, 164
Class structure, destruction of
old 85–8
reconstitution of new 129–33
See also Elite, emergent
Bolshevik.
Clergy 9, 88, 147, 148
Collective farms 102, 103
Commune (peasant) 11, 21, 42–3,
102
Constituent Assembly 19, 28, 38,
39, 43, 44–5, 49, 51, 90, 92
Constructivism 152
Cooperatives 80, 100, 101, 102–3
Corruption of state officials 69,
81, 119
Cossacks 47, 48
Counter-revolution 19, 33, 34,
86, 96
Cremation 146
Crime 96
juvenile 140, 142
Criminal Code (1922) 118
Cultural revolution 101, 144–7,
156
Czech Legion 49, 93
Crimea 26, 60

D

Defence Council 52, 75
Democracy 14, 15, 17, 19, 20, 31, 38, 39, 44–5
Democratic Centralists 68, 71
Denikin, A. I. 48, 52, 53, 54, 64
Deserters 48, 52, 82
Disease 9, 47
Disenfranchisement 131–3
Divorce 41, 138, 140
Doctors 9, 20, 134, 154
Domestic labour 138, 139
Don region 48, 53
Donbas 28, 30, 53, 93
Dovzhenko, A. 152
Drunkenness 108
Dual power 18–20
Duma 5, 6, 11,

E

Economy, crisis of 29–30, 72
Education 134–5, 141, 143
Eisenstein, S. 152
Elite, emergence of new 93, 116, 129, 137
Emigrés 86
Esenin, S. 143, 153
Estonia 26, 28, 48, 55

F

Factory committees 16, 29–30, 72, 107–8
   See also Worker's control of production
Family 137, 138, 139, 140, 141

F

Famine (1921–22) 82–3
Far Eastern Republic 122, 124
February Revolution 5–6, 14–15,
Fedin, K. 153
Finland 27, 48, 54, 55
Food requisitioning 76–7, 78, 79–80, 83, 89, 90, 100
Foremen 16, 105
First Five-Year Plan 106, 125, 162
First World War 12–14, 39, 47
   See also Peace, hopes for

G

Gastev, A. K. 106
Georgia 20, 27, 57, 61, 109, 122
Gentry 6–8, 11–12, 31, 42, 85, 86
Goloshchekin, F. I. 118
Grain supply 8, 29, 30, 72, 76, 102, 124–5
   See also Food requisitioning
Grechaninov, A. T. 87
Green movement 89.

H

Healthcare 134
Hooliganism 140, 143
Housing crisis 85, 91, 135–6, 143

I

Iaroslavskii, E. 149
Imperial family, execution of 49
Industry 6, 29, 83, 104–5
   cut in state subsidies to 100, 104; nationalization of 72,

Index

73, 85; planned development of 104, 112–13, 125

Intelligentsia 9, 86, 87, 123, 150–6

Ioffe, A. A. 41

Iudenich, N. N. 48, 95

Ivanov, V. 153

Izhevsk 92–3

J

Jews 12, 27, 56, 64, 149
  See also Anti-semitism

July Days 24–5, 32, 34.

K

Kadet party 19, 21, 25, 28, 31, 32, 44

Kamenev, L. B. 22, 24, 67, 109, 111, 115

Kandinsky, V. 151

Kautsky, K. 39

Kazakh SSR 61, 123

Kazakhs 26, 60–1, 82

Kerensky, A. F. 19, 22, 25, 32, 33, 35, 37

Khiva 26, 61

Khlebnikov, V. 151

Khorezm 61, 122

Kirov, S. M. 93, 118

Kokand 26, 61

Kolchak, A. V. 48, 51, 52, 53, 61, 64, 80, 93

Kollontai, A. M. 138, 140–1

Kombedy (committees of the rural poor) 65, 78–9

Komsomol (Communist Youth League) 106, 129, 134, 135, 142–3, 146, 149

Kornilov, L. G. 32–4, 38, 48

Krasin, L. B. 68

Kronstadt 16, 24, 86, 95–6, 100

Krupskaia, N. K. 15, 109, 135, 146

Kulaks 78, 89, 112, 120, 125, 126, 130, 131, 164

Kurds 124

L

Land Decree 40, 42–3, 44.

Land redistribution 30–1, 42–3, 76

Latvia 26, 27–8, 48, 55

Law in Soviet state 45, 49, 63, 64, 118

Lawyers 9, 17, 118

League of Militant Godless 149

Left Socialist Revolutionaries (SRs) 21, 22, 30, 34, 43, 63, 64, 66, 94, 160

Left Opposition 111, 113, 127

Lenin, V. I. 14, 16, 20, 25, 34–5, 41, 43, 44, 47, 55, 63, 71, 75, 98–9, 100, 109, 115, 122, 138, 141, 144, 162
  cult of 113, 149–50; economic policies espoused by 73, 83; on NEP 101; as party leader 67, 113, 126–7; personality of 22–3; *State and Revolution* 34, 95; testament of 109

Lewin, M. 163

Literacy 123, 138, 144–5

Literature 153–4

Lithuania 48, 56
Lunacharsky, A. V. 111, 135, 152
Lvov, G. E. 19, 22,

M

Makhno, N. I. 48, 56, 90
Malevich, K. S 151
Malia, M. 157
Mandelstam, O. 153
Mannerheim, K. G. 53
Marriage 137, 139
Martov, L. 95
Marxism 157–8
Mayakovsky, V. V. 137, 151
Mensheviks 5, 17, 20–1, 34, 38, 44, 45, 46, 57, 65, 92, 93, 94
Merchants 9, 10, 131
Meyerhold, V. Y. 151, 152
Middle classes 5, 9, 14, 86–7
     See also Service employees
Militarization of labour 72, 74, 82, 94
Military Revolutionary Committee (MRC) 35–6
Miliukov, P. N. 21–2,
Monetary inflation 14, 29, 82
     abolition of money 82;
          monetary stability restored 100
Moscow 34, 45, 46, 53, 64
Muslims 26, 60, 149
     Bashkirs 60; Tatars 26, 60, 89, 124

N

Nation, discourse of 32, 167

Nation-building in 1920s 122–4
Nationalists, non-Russian 26–8, 44, 47, 54, 55–61
Nepmen 131
Nicholas II 6, 12, 13, 15,
Nomenklatura. See Elite, emergence of new.

O

October Manifesto (1905) 11
October seizure of power 35–8, 40, 87
Old Believers 148
Omsk 17, 51, 53
One-person management 74, 105
Order No. 1 16.
Ordzhonikidze, G. K. 118

P

Partisans 47, 48
Pasternak, B. L. 47
Patriarchy 108, 139, 162
Peace, hopes for 14, 21, 39, 41–2, 44.
Peace Decree 40, 41.
Peasants 6–8, 17–18, 20, 27, 30–1, 38, 45, 103, 119–22, 127, 142, 147
     class differentiation among 77–9, 130; uprisings against Bolsheviks 48, 89–90
     See also Commune; Land redistribution; Kombedy; Kulaks
Petliura, S. V. 64

Petrograd (St Petersburg, Leningrad) 8–9, 10, 143
Petrograd Soviet of Workers' and Soldiers' Deputies 5, 16, 18–19, 21, 34, 38
Pilniak, V. 153
Pilsudski, J. 54
Pipes, R. 162
Poland 27, 48, 56, 61
  Soviet-Polish war 56
Population 8, 47, 85
Preobrazhensky, E. 160
Productivity 72, 73–4, 105–6
Prostitution 141
Provisional Government 5, 15, 19, 20, 21, 26–8, 29, 55
  coalition government 22,
Publishing 9,
Pudovkin, V. 152

Q
Queuing 137

R
Rabkrin. See Workers' and Peasants' Inspectorate
Radek, K. B. 55, 167
Rakovsky, C. G. 122
Rasputin, G. Ye. 13,
Rationing 80–1, 91, 93, 94, 124
Red Army 47, 48, 55, 57, 66, 76, 91, 134, 145
  causes of victory of 51–4, 94;
  'military specialists' 49, 52;
Red Guards 37, 44, 46, 48, 92
Red Terror 62, 63–4, 118

Religious sects 143–4, 148
Renovationists 148
Revolution of 1905 5, 6
Riga, Treaty of 56
Right Opposition 112, 115
Riutin, M. I. 115
Rodchenko, A.M. 151
Roslavets, N. 151
RSFSR (All-Russian Socialist Federal Soviet Republic) 64, 109, 122
Rykov, A. I. 111
Russian Social Democratic and Labour Party 5, 10, 20
  See also Bolshevik party, Mensheviks

S
Sailors 15, 24, 95–6
Samara 46, 89, 92, 144
Saratov 45
Scientific organization of labour (NOT) 106, 156
'Scissors crisis 100, 111
Service employees 108, 129, 137
Sexual revolution 140
Shklovsky, V. B. 85
Smithy group of writers 153
Siberia 45, 53, 77, 80, 82, 90
Social estates 9
Socialist Revolutionaries (SRs) 10, 17, 20–1, 38, 39, 42, 44, 45, 46, 64, 65, 90, 92, 94
  the 'democratic counter-revolution' 48, 49–51, 92–3

See also Left Socialist
    Revolutionaries
Soviets 17, 34, 43, 45, 65, 162
    Central Executive Committee
      (CEC) of 17, 34, 35, 43, 46,
      66, 80, 100; in countryside
      17, 45–6, 119–20; demand
      for power to 34, 35, 43,
      44–5, 90, 97, 164;
      opposition to Bolshevik
      regime 46;
    See also Petrograd Soviet
Sport 134
Sovnarkom (Council of People's
    Commissars) 43, 46, 66, 111
Spiridonova, M. A. 64
SR Maximalists 46, 92
Stalin, I.V. 22, 55, 67, 101, 109,
    111–13, 122, 123, 125, 126, 127–
    8, 149, 155, 158, 161
    personality of 115; and
      'socialism in one country'
      111, 113–14; Stalinism 161–2,
      163
Steinberg, I. N. 63
Stolypin, P. A. 11, 102
Strikes 5, 10–11, 15. 29, 31, 93–4,
    107
Students 5, 142
Suicide 143
Sultangaliev, M. S. 60, 123
Supreme Economic Council
    (Sovnarkhoz) 72, 75, 86, 104
Sverdlov, Ia. M. 67,

T

Tadzhik SSR 61

Tambov 90
Tashkent 61
Tatlin, V. Y. 151
Tax in kind 100, 101–2
Teachers 9, 17, 20, 135, 154
Technical specialists (*spetsy*) 74,
    105, 131, 154
Theatre 152
Tikhon (V. I. Beliavin) 87–8, 147,
    148
Tolstoy, L. N. 18
Tomsky, M. P. 75, 112,
Trade, ban on 72, 80, 137
    free trade restored 100, 131
Trade unions 10, 16–17, 65, 93,
    105, 107
    Bolshevik policy towards 74,
      162
Transportation, crisis in 29, 72,
    76, 83
Trotsky, L.D. 10, 24, 25, 35, 37, 38,
    41, 48, 67, 74, 75, 81, 82, 109,
    111, 112, 113, 114, 115, 127, 161,
    162
Tsereteli, I. G. 21, 25.
Turkestan. *See* Central Asia
Tukhachevsky, M. N. 52
Turkmen SSR 61, 145
Tver' 46, 117

U

Ukraine 27, 28, 31, 44, 47, 54, 56,
    64, 82, 90, 102, 122, 123
    See also Donbas
Ukrainian Communist Party 56,
    123

Unemployment 29, 92, 107, 140, 143

United Opposition 111, 112

Universities 9, 142, 155

Urals 10, 26, 30, 45, 53

USSR (1923-) 62, 122, 123-4

Uzbek SSR 61

V

Vertov, D. 152, 154

W

War, policy on 21-2, 39
revolutionary defencism 16, 24

War scare (1927) 124

Whites 47, 48, 51-4, 83, 93
White programme 53-4;
White terror 64

Women 5, 20, 44, 106, 107, 119, 137-41, 142, 143, 145, 165
See also Patriarchy

Women's Bureau 138-9, 141

Workers 5, 10, 15, 16-17, 21, 28, 29-30, 31, 38, 90-1, 106-9, 137, 165
oppose Bolsheviks 68, 92-5, 108; wages of 91, 92, 106
See also Labour productivity;
Militarization of labour;
Strikes

Workers' control of production 29-30, 40, 72-3, 90, 97
See also One-person management

Workers' and Peasants' Inspectorate 117

Workers' Opposition 68, 75

Wrangel, P. N. 47, 51, 52

Y

Youth 141-4, 147, 165

Z

Zalkind, A. B. 141

Zemstvos 14, 19, 20, 119

Zinoviev, G. E. 24, 35, 67, 69, 80, 109, 111, 112, 115

Zoshchenko, M. 153

Expand your collection of
VERY SHORT INTRODUCTIONS

Available now

1. Classics
2. Music
3. Buddhism
4. Literary Theory
5. Hinduism
6. Psychology
7. Islam
8. Politics
9. Theology
10. Archaeology
11. Judaism
12. Sociology
13. The Koran
14. The Bible
15. Social and Cultural Anthropology
16. History
17. Roman Britain
18. The Anglo-Saxon Age
19. Medieval Britain
20. The Tudors
21. Stuart Britain
22. Eighteenth-Century Britain
23. Nineteenth-Century Britain
24. Twentieth-Century Britain
25. Heidegger
26. Ancient Philosophy
27. Socrates
28. Marx
29. Logic
30. Descartes
31. Machiavelli
32. Aristotle
33. Hume
34. Nietzsche
35. Darwin
36. The European Union
37. Gandhi
38. Augustine
39. Intelligence
40. Jung
41. Buddha
42. Paul
43. Continental Philosophy
44. Galileo
45. Freud
46. Wittgenstein
47. Indian Philosophy
48. Rousseau
49. Hegel
50. Kant
51. Cosmology
52. Drugs
53. Russian Literature
54. The French Revolution
55. Philosophy
56. Barthes
57. Animal Rights
58. Kierkegaard
59. Russell
60. Shakespeare
61. Clausewitz
62. Schopenhauer
63. The Russian Revolution
64. Hobbes

Visit the
VERY SHORT
INTRODUCTIONS
Web site

www.oup.co.uk/vsi

➤ **Information** about all published titles

➤ News of **forthcoming books**

➤ **Extracts** from the books, including titles
  not yet published

➤ **Reviews** and views

➤ **Links** to other **web sites** and main
  OUP web page

➤ Information about **VSIs in translation**

➤ **Contact** the editors

➤ **Order** other **VSIs** on-line